DEMONSTRATING

STUDENT

MASTERY

with Digital Badges and Portfolios

DEMONSTRATING

STUDENT

MASTERY

with Digital Badges and Portfolios

David Niguidula

Alexandria, VA USA

1703 N. Beauregard St. • Alexandria, VA 22311-1714 USA
Phone: 800-933-2723 or 703-578-9600 • Fax: 703-575-5400
Website: www.ascd.org • E-mail: member@ascd.org
Author guidelines: www.ascd.org/write

Deborah S. Delisle, *Executive Director;* Stefani Roth, *Publisher;* Genny Ostertag, *Director, Content Acquisitions;* Allison Scott, *Acquisitions Editor;* Julie Houtz, *Director, Book Editing & Production;* Liz Wegner, *Editor;* Judi Connelly, *Associate Art Director;* Thomas Lytle, *Senior Graphic Designer;* Valerie Younkin, *Production Designer;* Mike Kalyan, *Director, Production Services;* Shajuan Martin, *E-Publishing Specialist;* Kelly Marshall, *Senior Production Specialist*

PAPERBACK ISBN: 978-1-4166-2706-7   ASCD product #119026   n1/19
PDF E-BOOK ISBN: 978-1-4166-2729-6; see Books in Print for other formats.
Quantity discounts are available: e-mail programteam@ascd.org or call 800-933-2723, ext. 5773, or 703-575-5773. For desk copies, go to www.ascd.org/deskcopy.

Library of Congress Cataloging-in-Publication Data
Names: Niguidula, David A., author.
Title: Demonstrating student mastery with digital badges and portfolios / David Niguidula.
Description: Alexandria, VA : ASCD, [2019] | Includes bibliographical references and index.
Identifiers: LCCN 2018039464 (print) | LCCN 2018055322 (ebook) | ISBN 9781416627296 (PDF) | ISBN 9781416627067 (pbk.)
Subjects: LCSH: Digital badges. | Portfolios in education. | Student-centered learning. | Internet in education.
Classification: LCC LB1028.72 (ebook) | LCC LB1028.72 .N54 2019 (print) | DDC 371.33--dc23
LC record available at https://lccn.loc.gov/2018039464

28 27 26 25 24 23 22 21 20 19   1 2 3 4 5 6 7 8 9 10 11 12

DEMONSTRATING
STUDENT
MASTERY
with Digital Badges and Portfolios

Foreword

With perfect timing, *Demonstrating Student Mastery with Digital Badges and Portfolios* has arrived to assist the burgeoning number of educators standing at the intersection of personalized learning and digital documentation. Throughout the nation and world, teachers and administrators are searching for meaningful ways to collect exemplars of student learning and provide responsive feedback. More importantly, questions are emerging about how to involve students in collecting these meaningful artifacts, reflecting on what they reveal, and taking action to propel their learning journey. Certainly, there are and have been many outstanding professionals engaged in determining the best way to select and compile portfolio collections over the years. There is in my view, however, one educator who stands out as the pioneer and the most knowledgeable person I know in the field of digital portfolios design: Dr. David Niguidula. As a visionary in his initial work at Brown University with Ted Sizer's Coalition of Essential Schools in the 1980s, David saw the power of integrating digital sharing with its immediate access and ease of compilation with the incentive to have students "own" their learning and monitor their pathway to mastery.

With his technology know-how and pedagogical understanding, David was ready to respond when the Rhode Island Department of Education determined that it would require a digital portfolio of learners as a graduation requirement. David and his organization stepped up by creating an online platform, Richer Picture, to engage school faculties with learners to begin to build a body of work reflecting each child's journey. The platform has been and continues to be an active presence throughout the nation and overseas as an easy to navigate yet sophisticated model for engaging whole schools and systems. The range of the platform's use and the years behind its development have in turn provided David with exceptionally unique experience that backs up the strategies and insights he shares in the book. He truly knows how to engage professionals in co-creating with their students a vibrant collection of work that authentically shows the learner's journey.

I recall seeing a Rhode Island 1st grader, Carlene, working hard reading through a short story, demonstrating her ability to sound out words in the story. Recently David shared Carlene's graduation portfolio where she was presenting a TED-style talk about what makes a "true" education. Rhode Island was the beginning, but David has uncovered best practices, having worked with thousands of educators, observing the nuances of motivation and the power of feedback for learners of all ages.

David's work has had and continues to have a significant influence in my professional life. He has been a trusted colleague in my work on curriculum mapping that supports big picture vertical and cross-grade level connections in K–12 using electronic platforms. Portfolio reviews are instrumental in considering how to inform curriculum maps with evidence of student work in order to address gaps in planning. What's more, we share a commitment to modernizing choices for curriculum and assessment to meet the needs of today's learners. Our young students know what century they are living in and do not wish to be time traveling backward when they enter a school building. Given the active and prominent role of students in David's badge and portfolio selection process, there is a constant opportunity to rethink curricular and assessment choices to craft them as contemporary.

With these years and years of experience, David has written the exceptional book in your hands (or on your screen) to assist you and your colleagues at all levels wishing to launch a digital portfolio program that has fidelity to the learner. He has shaped power in the digital portfolio as a place not only to collect evidence of how students are growing and meeting challenges but most importantly to "show who the student is as an individual learner." The integrity of his work is evident throughout the book. David is sincerely committed to documenting the authentic journey of our learners.

The title, *Demonstrating Student Mastery with Digital Badges and Portfolios,* goes straight to the fundamental purpose of the book: Human beings need feedback to monitor learning. To know if we are moving toward mastery of proficiencies and knowledge that are of importance to us, we need clear striking signals. Hence the focus on badges is central to involving students directly in stepping back and reflecting on their learning journey. Given school settings where they move year to year under the care of many teachers, the need for portfolio collections is utterly essential to see the big picture.

Perhaps the timeliest outcome of the book is how it operationalizes *personalized learning,* which has become a desired goal but often meanders in definitions and vagueness when it comes time for implementation. What David has developed is a process of genuinely engaging student *voice* in the *choice* of setting goals, selecting work, receiving feedback, earning badges, and setting new targets. We are fortunate to have the practical and inspirational *Demonstrating Student Mastery with Digital Badges and Portfolios* to guide creative educators on how to launch and sustain efforts to help our learners navigate their futures.

—Heidi Hayes Jacobs

Introduction

Schools are being asked to become more personalized and more standardized—simultaneously. To respond, some schools set up one initiative to focus on achievement and then another initiative to get to know students individually. All too often, these initiatives end up competing for time or even conflicting with each other. This book outlines how it's possible to do both. Students *can* meet standards while, at the same time, show who they are as individuals. And they can do this through the use of digital badges and digital portfolios.

A Few Quick Definitions

Digital badges are a visual way of representing accomplishments. This book focuses on badges that are earned by students (although the same process can be applied to badges earned by teachers).

Typically, a school can start defining badges by examining what every student should know and be able to do. Students can earn badges in all areas of school life: academic areas (writing, mathematics, the arts, world languages), extracurricular activities (community service, athletics, theater), and other areas (habits of mind, work habits).

Students earn badges by completing requirements; for example, a student can earn a writing badge by submitting examples of different genres of writing (persuasive writing, fiction, narrative, etc.). The "digital" part of the badge means that the information about the badge is stored online.

Digital portfolios are an online collection of student work that demonstrates the student's accomplishments as a learner. Students submit work to their portfolio online; the work can take many forms (classroom assignments, projects, reading logs, after-school activities) and can be in any format (word-processed documents, spreadsheets, audio, video, images, websites, podcasts).

To be more than just an electronic file cabinet, digital portfolios need to be used as a form of assessment and reflection. Students can collect, select, and present the work in the portfolio as evidence that they have met the badge requirements. Teachers can then use online tools to approve the student submission and verify that the student has met the criteria to earn the badge.

Digital portfolios can be structured in many ways. In this book, a portfolio is a collection of badges. In turn, each badge contains student evidence and teachers' verification.

Mastery refers to students achieving a certain level of accomplishment before moving on to the next unit or course. *Competencies* are the set of skills, knowledge, and habits that we expect students to master. For the purposes of what you're about to read, *competencies, proficiencies, expectations,* and *standards* are essentially interchangeable. Mastery learning (also known as competency-based or proficiency-based learning) is a model of schooling that focuses on students achieving the necessary competencies at their own pace.

Taken together, digital badges and portfolios provide a means for both personalizing and mastering the competencies. A student portfolio can consist of two sets of badges: the *required* badges, representing the competencies expected of all students, and the *personal* badges, representing the student's areas of interest. The specific evidence in the portfolio and the combination of badges that the student earns give a richer picture of that student's achievement. In the final view, a portfolio shows how the student has met the competencies—and it also shows who the student is as a learner.

A Roadmap for Readers

Think of this book as a guide through the stages of the implementation process. The chapters are organized in the order in which most schools get started. You can think of these stages as a rough guide to your first year of implementation. Each chapter addresses one or more *essential questions* to help you frame the conversation at your school.

Overview

Setting the vision: What does mastery look like? What can portfolios tell us about students as learners and as individuals? Chapter 1 explores the various ways digital portfolios and badges are being used to both demonstrate student achievement and provide personalized feedback. The schools that have had the most success with implementing and sustaining portfolios are the ones that have a clearly defined purpose. If you are wondering whether portfolios are worth the effort, this chapter provides reasons that educators have found most compelling.

Before the School Year Begins

Defining badges: What do we want our students to know and be able to do? At the beginning, schools need to define the badges and expectations. What is our vision of what we want students to know and be able to do? What will that look like? Contradictory as it sounds, we begin by thinking about the end. Creating a common vision of what we expect for each student—and articulating that vision as a set of badges—is a driving force for the rest of the work. Chapter 2 discusses this at greater length.

The Beginning of the School Year

Aligning assessments: How do students earn the badges? What goes into the portfolio? How do we create portfolio-worthy tasks? With the school's vision in mind, teachers need to consider what opportunities students will have to earn these badges. This process can build on what teachers are already doing and open a conversation about what teachers want students to carry away from their classes. As teachers think about their current assignments, many schools use this as an opportunity to design some new assessments. Perhaps there hasn't been as much emphasis on group work in one grade level; this could be the catalyst to try something new. It's also the opportunity to open things up to students. What might they consider their best work? What might they do outside school? Where are the opportunities for personalization, and what do we do about standardized testing? These questions are the focus of Chapter 3.

Throughout the School Year

Feedback, rubrics, and assessment: How do we decide what's good—or, at least, good enough? As the school year progresses, there's a regular cycle of interaction. At certain points of the year, students work on their projects or assignments. This is where they're creating the elements for their portfolios. Students may need varying levels of guidance in this creation, but in the end, we should see the student work that shows the student's current level of achievement.

Teachers, in turn, provide feedback to the students by assessing the work. Chapter 4 examines how common rubrics can help ensure a level of "standards without standardization." That is, schools can set things up so there is a common understanding of what work is considered "good enough." The development of rubrics and a calibration protocol are crucial for ensuring a fair assessment. When done well, it can actually allow for greater possibilities; if students come up with their own ideas and projects that they want to submit to the portfolio, the common rubrics make it possible to assess the work and ensure a similar level of quality, whether the work was done in or out of school.

The End of the School Year

Tours: How do students present their best work? Toward the end of the year (or term), students will present their portfolios. They can do a tour of their portfolios; that is, they can curate the elements within the portfolio and determine which pieces are the best ones to present; then they can captivate their audience by showing how they're meeting standards—while showing who they are as individuals. The tours are an opportunity to look at the body of work; as such, they enable students and teachers to consider patterns of strength or weakness. The tours are also a chance to put the work in context. Is it clear how each individual assignment or student project links to the larger vision? These tours will be the focus of Chapter 5.

Reflecting on the Year and Moving Forward

School culture: How do we make sure the portfolios are valued? How do we build on what we already have? What else has to change? School leaders often ask how to get buy-in. Whether that buy-in is from teachers, students, parents, or other community members, the champions of the cause want to know how to move from "initiative" to a routine part of school life. The fact is, portfolios can build on your school's current best practices, the most meaningful assignments that your teachers give *now,* and the interactions that your students find most supportive.

The potential of digital badges and portfolios is to provide a deeper conversation. To determine what will be valuable, the portfolios have to provide new information or insights. At the end of your first cycle, teachers and students might note that there are things they want to describe about their work that currently aren't in the portfolio or aren't represented by a badge. This is a good thing. The process of revising to reflect what the community finds truly important is what gives an initiative staying power. Chapter 6 discusses this effect on school culture.

Resources That Can Help

Your school doesn't need to start from scratch. Many schools have worked on digital portfolios and badges over the years. At the very end of the book, the Appendix contains an array of supporting documents organized into two broad categories for easy reference: (1) sample badge lists and (2) badge tour templates and rubrics. These documents can help guide your thinking as you begin to create your own materials that will work best for your school community.

1

Setting the Vision

What does mastery look like?

What can portfolios tell us about students as learners and as individuals?

On a day in June, a 9th grader named Amanda sat down with two teachers for her end-of-year review. Ms. C had been Amanda's social studies teacher. Mr. G didn't know Amanda because his science classes were typically taken by 10th and 11th graders. These two were teamed together because they came from different grade levels and departments and could provide different perspectives, but the school guaranteed that each student would have a familiar face on the review team. After everyone settled in, Ms. C asked Amanda to log in and open her digital portfolio.

On the opening screen, displayed in Figure 1.1, the teachers could see Amanda's progress shown as a set of digital badges.

At Amanda's school, the badges are divided into two categories. The top row lists the schoolwide badges; these represent the competencies that every student should master. On her first day of school, Amanda learned about her school's vision for what it would mean to graduate—what every student who walks across the stage should know and be able to do. Whenever Amanda or any of her classmates open their portfolios, they see the badges that represent the school's competencies—that is, the specific academic, social, and career-readiness goals that every graduate should possess. Each student uses the digital portfolio to document his or her progress toward that vision.

FIGURE 1.1 | **Amanda's Badges**

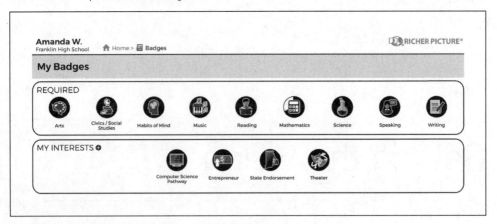

The bottom row of badges represents how Amanda personalizes her education. These badges represent the pursuit of her particular interests: Amanda is in the process of completing the school's pathway in computer science, and she has participated in after-school activities for entrepreneurship and theater. She is also pursuing a state endorsement in BiLiteracy, meaning she needs to demonstrate proficiency in two languages; her state has defined several endorsements that can be attached to a student's diploma if the student completes specific requirements in an academic, career, or technical field. The badges in this row come from both elective courses that Amanda selects and the activities that Amanda participates in (both in and out of school). Although every student at Amanda's school has the same top row, each student will have a different combination of badges in the bottom row.

Throughout the year, Amanda added work to her portfolio; most of it was from her class assignments and projects, but some was from outside class. Each piece of work she added was connected to one or more of the school's competencies. If the work was approved by a teacher, then it could count as a step toward earning the badge. Some badges have detailed requirements. For example, to earn the writing badge, every student needs to submit samples of persuasive, narrative, and reflective essays. The requirements for other badges might have choices built in; to earn the arts badge, Amanda could choose to complete the requirements in music, theater, or visual arts.

At this point, we can see that Amanda has completed many of her badges at the bronze level for this year because the badge is entirely filled in. (In this case, the bronze category refers to an introductory level of competency.) Notice, though, that the math badge is only partially filled in, indicating that the work is still in progress.

As Ms. C and Mr. G looked at the badges, they talked with Amanda about her overall progress: What did she find hard? What was she most proud of? Then they turned from the general to the specific.

Since September, Amanda had added two or three entries from each of her classes, meaning she had more than a dozen entries from the year. For this session, however, Amanda selected four particular entries that she wanted to share with Ms. C and Mr. G. As she brought each piece of work to the screen—a short story from English, a complex algebra problem, a civics project looking at voting patterns, a portrait of her brother—she explained why she thought these pieces were her best pieces from the year. The teachers prompted her occasionally, asking about how a particular entry connected to the school's expectations or asking her to provide more detail about a given assignment. For the most part, though, the teachers just let Amanda talk. A soft-spoken student, Amanda began by talking more to the screen than to the teachers. But by the end of the session—just 15 minutes later—she was looking directly at the teachers and describing her overall sense of what she had accomplished this year.

At another school, Robert, a 12th grader, was preparing his own presentation. He had just finished spending eight months working on his senior year capstone project. His panel included two teachers, the assistant principal, and a community member (who had been a mentor to other students' capstones). His project focused on environmental issues—specifically, how the shrimp and shellfish population near his New England community had been devastated in recent years.

During his presentation, Robert described how he had found a local researcher who was studying how to repopulate the shellfish breeding grounds. He projected pictures from his portfolio that showed him on the beach with the research team, learning how to identify and count the spawning generations; he also had prepared graphs and charts that showed the change in the shellfish population over time and what the researchers hoped to accomplish in the future. When he was done, the teachers asked him some detailed questions about the work, about the research paper he had written, and about what he believed was his "learning stretch."

In a third location, a younger student, Sasha, was getting ready for her student-led conference. As a 5th grader, she had done this before; her parents and her teacher were sitting together before a laptop at her desk. Sasha started by talking about the work that displayed her strength as a learner. She ran a video from math class that showed her standing at a whiteboard, describing a word problem. As the clip played on the computer, the group watched Sasha identify the most important information, come up with an equation, and generate the answer. The teacher noted that Sasha's entry was a part of the "problem-solving" badge. (Although Sasha's entry for that badge had focused on fractions, other students had earned the badge by explaining how to find the lowest common denominator or how to create different graphs from weather data to test a hypothesis.) Next, Sasha talked about the work that made her proud, a piece of writing that had required several drafts before she was happy with it. She was able to pull up her previous writing and note the differences between what she had done before and what she was doing now.

A Better Conversation

Digital portfolios and badges are a means to an end. The end, in this case, is the kind of conversation that all three of these students had with their teachers and parents. Consider Amanda's discussion with Ms. C and Mr. G. For 15 minutes, this 9th grader was the center of attention. She had the chance to talk about her accomplishments with teachers whose job at that moment was to help her reflect on her skills. The questions before the teachers were general ones that all schools care about: Is this student meeting our expectations? Is she on track to move to 10th grade and on to graduation?

For this session, however, the question was about one specific student: Is *Amanda* meeting our expectations? When the question is personalized— when the student is sitting face to face with a teacher—the question about meeting standards and mastery moves from an anonymous yes/no judgment to a conversation about how to help Amanda advance to the next level. This is the end this school has in mind: allowing Amanda to receive specific, personalized feedback about her work and concrete suggestions about how she can move forward.

Not incidentally, this approach uses technology, specifically, digital badges and portfolios. Our work in digital portfolios extends back to the 1990s (Niguidula, 1993; 1997), when many schools were just beginning to use e-mail and word processors and very few had local networks, let alone connections to the internet. In those early days, a great deal of time was required for students and teachers to get familiar with the necessary technology tools to save files on a network or create a digital video. Technological advances have greatly reduced the learning curve to use any platform, and current portfolio and badge platforms give great power to students and teachers as they create, organize, and communicate about their work. But through the years, we have learned a crucial lesson: When schools think of implementing digital portfolios as primarily a technology initiative (as opposed to a personalization or assessment initiative), they will have a more difficult time. We have learned that the best educational technology projects start with the *education*, rather than the *technology*. In this age of accountability, where educators feel they spend hours upon hours focusing on complying with state mandates, digital portfolios offer a refreshing alternative. The portfolio is a representation of what's happening in the student's world; the student entries are typically either responses to assignments created by the teacher or projects initiated by the student. The portfolio can cover the full range of what we want a student to know and be able to do—not just the limited standards that are measured by standardized tests. The badges within the portfolio can represent the wide range of experiences that students have each year. The portfolio is an opportunity for students to create work, curate what they have done, and captivate an audience with their accomplishments and growth over time.

What Is a Digital Portfolio?

A digital portfolio is more than a collection of student work. The portfolio needs to have a purpose, something that will help the student figure out what to put into the portfolio and let any reader of the portfolio know what to expect. Specifically, *the portfolio needs to contain evidence that a student is mastering a set of expectations, while at the same time showing who the student is as an individual learner.*

The goals provide the structure of the portfolio; the individuality comes in as students select the pieces they want to put into the portfolio. Let's look at four types of portfolios from different grade levels. (Note that you can see a number of these examples in more detail in the Appendix.)

Best Work Portfolios

One easy way that schools get started is by asking students to select their best work. For example, an elementary school portfolio could structure its digital portfolio as shown in Figure 1.2.

FIGURE 1.2 | **Elementary School Badges**

To get ready for your student-led conference, please include your best work from this term. Each entry should have a reflection that answers the question "What does this entry say about me as a learner?"		
	Reading	My Work * Reflection
	Writing	My Work * Reflection
	Math	My Work * Reflection
	Social Studies	My Work * Reflection
	Science	My Work * Reflection
	Phys Ed/Health	My Work * Reflection
	Music	My Work * Reflection
	My Choice (Select an entry that shows how you grew as a learner, and explain why.)	My Work * Reflection

Essentially, the student is asked to select a best piece from each subject area; clicking on the "My Work" link in the right column then leads the portfolio's reader to the actual student entry. Because the portfolio is digital, the student entries can be in any medium—audio, video, presentations, word-processed documents, images, and so on. If the student originally did the work on paper, a quick picture taken with a smartphone or tablet can capture the work digitally and ready it for upload.

At one school, the portfolios were prepared twice a year for parent conferences. For the youngest students, the Reading entry contained a video of the child doing an independent reading. We can see the student open the book and tell us the title, and we watch as she moves through the words. Does the student read fluidly, or are there points where she struggles? When a word is unfamiliar, does she look for clues in the context or in the illustrations? If the student is asked questions about the reading, does she show that she understood the text?

Video is a powerful medium; as we watch, we can take in a great deal of information. We can watch the student's body language and see where she looks confident and where she seems unsure. We can also hear the pauses when she's trying to figure out a sound, and we can sense the relief when she gets it. Clips as short as 30–60 seconds can give parents a strong sense of a student's abilities.

The portfolio can also let the student focus on a particular skill or ability. For example, one school wanted to put more emphasis on problem-solving skills in math. In one class, students started doing problems of the week—open-ended word problems that required a little more analysis to solve. Students collected their work in a binder. For the digital portfolio presentation, they selected one of their pieces. The teacher then asked the student to walk through the problem and answer three questions: Can you tell me what this problem is about? What do you need to do to solve the problem? Can you show me your math work? This interview was then captured on video. In this case, what's significant is that the teacher used the portfolio to focus on a particular skill rather than on specific content. It didn't matter that one student's problem was about fractions and another's was about measurement. The focus was on the problem-solving process; allowing the student to select the specific problem for the interview gave the student a voice in what the portfolio was going to look like.

Not all entries need to be on video; plenty of portfolio entries are done with paper and pencil (or pen, marker, or crayon). What good portfolio entries tend to have in common is that they are *performances* of some kind. The performance may be brief, but it's a way of showing more than a typical recall-based quiz or test can show. The student is demonstrating his or her skills and knowledge.

Now let's consider a high school example. Figure 1.3 shows a list of what a student must demonstrate to graduate. Students need to have one sample in each category. Some work samples could fit more than one expectation, but students at this school need to have a different sample for each expectation.

FIGURE 1.3 | **Secondary School Badge Requirements**

Expectation	Requirement	Work Sample	Completed
Acquire, analyze, and evaluate information and ideas to effectively solve problems.			
1.1	Acquire and apply knowledge and skills within and across the curriculum.	--	
1.2	Work actively and cooperatively to achieve group goals.	My Work	★
1.3	Apply problem-solving strategies.	--	
1.4	Synthesize information from multiple sources and formats to complete authentic learning tasks.	--	
Communicate information clearly and effectively using a variety of 21st century skills.			
2.1	Demonstrate an understanding of texts.	--	
2.2	Write clearly and concisely.	My Work	★
2.3	Speak, listen, and interpret effectively.	--	
2.4	Communicate through an art form (visual, music, dance, drama, graphics).	--	
Value and demonstrate personal and social responsibility.			
3.1	Make informed life and career decisions (ILP) (each year).	--	
3.2	Recognize and respect the diversity, cultures, and individuality of others.	--	
3.3	Participate in community service, leadership roles, and/or school activities.	--	
3.4	Make appropriate choices affecting one's wellness that contribute to a healthy lifestyle.	--	
Use digital tools to access, evaluate, and effectively apply information.			
4.1	Use technological tools to access information.	My Work	★
4.2	Use technological tools to evaluate information.	--	
4.3	Use technological tools to communicate information.	--	

Source: Burrillville High School, Harrisville, Rhode Island. Used with permission.

This school's requirements are not simply about academics. There are four broad categories that ask the student to demonstrate how he or she can "acquire, analyze, and evaluate information," "communicate information clearly and effectively," "demonstrate personal responsibility" and "use digital tools." These categories are each further divided into three or four specific expectations.

The right-most column in the table is marked "Completed" and is represented by a badge. For a student to earn that badge, a teacher has to sign off. The school has developed schoolwide rubrics for each of the expectations; using that rubric, each student entry needs to receive a "meets expectation" or better rating (in this case, a "3" or better on a 4-point scale).

Most of the student entries come from classroom assignments. Each teacher in the school has identified three or four "portfolio-worthy" tasks from each full-year class. These specific portfolio assignments are associated with one or more of the expectations; thus, students know if they do well on this assignment, they will be able to earn one of the badges. Students at this school carry a typical course load of five or six classes; because there are four tasks in each class, over four years, students will have up to 80–100 opportunities to earn badges.

Since the expectations are broad, they're not limited to a specific subject area. To demonstrate expectation 2.3—"speak, listen, and interpret effectively"—one student could include a traditional oral report from an English class, another student might use a debate from social studies, and a third could show coaching skills that she uses with younger members of the basketball team. This list of requirements deliberately does not indicate *where* the student has to demonstrate these skills; the tasks could come from any class—all teachers are expected to have tasks and score them using the common rubrics. The school has turned the portfolio and expectations into a true schoolwide endeavor. Individual teachers are still focused on their specific classrooms and curricula, but now there is a common point of conversation. Everyone in the school community uses the schoolwide expectations as a reference point for their work. (For schools that have developed curriculum maps, this set of common expectations can provide a key point of analysis when doing a map walkthrough. Chapter 6 explores this idea in more detail.)

Subject Portfolios

A portfolio can also be structured around goals within a specific subject area. For example, a writing portfolio could ask a student to complete entries that show each genre (see Figure 1.4).

FIGURE 1.4 | **Writing Portfolio Contents**

	To complete your writing badge, you must meet each of the requirements listed below.	
Met	**Genre**	**My Work**
☑	Research Paper	Final Draft Research Paper
☑	Response to Literature	The Stand: Literary Criticism
☑	Creative Work (original story or poetry)	Original Myth
☑	Persuasive Essay	The Crucible Essay
☑	Reflective Writing	Transcendentalism Assignment

This school has identified five genres; students need to select their best example of each. The portfolio could well contain more than one example for any one of the genres. The student might collect the pieces over, say, the last two years of elementary school or the first two years of high school and decide at different points which Response to Literature was currently his "best."

Each school has to determine its own definition of what makes an entry acceptable. In this case, do the samples need to come from English class? Do they need to come from school at all, or is a screenplay or story the student wrote outside school acceptable?

Similarly, other curricular areas can define portfolios, as we will see in Chapter 2. From math to art, from physical education to career and technical areas, subject portfolios can contain the evidence containing the most essential skills, knowledge, and habits.

Project-Based Portfolios

Student voice is a crucial component of any successful portfolio system. One great way that schools can begin to personalize learning is to encourage students to participate in project-based learning.

Most schools already engage in some level of project-based learning, typically through some existing structure, such as science fairs or model United Nations. An increasing number of schools are going further and establishing capstone projects, in which every student creates an independent project representing a learning stretch in an area of their own interest, or follow project structures, such as the Buck Institute for Education's "Gold Standard" (Larmer, Mergendroller, & Boss, 2015b) or the quests as defined in *The Quest for Learning* (Alcock, Fisher, & Zmuda, 2018)

A digital portfolio, in this case, lets the student track progress through the steps of the project (see Figure 1.5).

FIGURE 1.5 | **Capstone Project: Portfolio Contents**

Capstone Project		
Milestone	**Link to My Work**	**Approved**
Proposal: letter of intent and project goals	My Work	☑
Preliminary topic and central questions	My Work	☑
Sign of commitment	My Work	☑
Fieldwork log	My Work	☑
Journal entries	My Work	☑
Mentor responses	My Work	☑
Research paper	My Work	In progress
Overall reflection		
Final presentation		
Evaluation	Self-Evaluation	Reviewer Evaluation

Source: Narragansett High School, Narragansett, Rhode Island. Used with permission.

Here, the structure of the portfolio is organized around the project milestones. Over the course of the year, the student will complete these tasks and move closer toward earning the project badge.

The key to this kind of portfolio is flexibility. At the beginning, the student establishes specific goals that the project will meet. The school has created the project milestones to provide a general framework, but the student's proposal will identify exactly how those milestones will be met. For example, a student's project focused on ocean science research will probably involve fieldwork in a lab or at the beach, whereas another student's project on dance will involve studio time.

Entries for the project portfolio are added as the student goes through the year; they typically aren't put in all at the end. The actual evidence can include photos or videos of the work in the field (such as photos of collecting specimens for the ocean research project or images from a rehearsal for the dance project), as well as written pieces, such as journal entries, as the student moves through the project. Again, the specific form will depend on the student's choice.

A digital portfolio enables a school to keep track of these myriad conditions. Next to each milestone, the student submits a link to his work. Each submission is reviewed; when it's approved, the student moves to the next stage. In the end, the student submits a self-evaluation, describing how the project has met the goals that he set, while the teacher (or other reviewers) gives a final evaluation and (hopefully) approval.

In this case, the digital portfolio helps schools expand their boundaries. The goals and topic are generated by the student; the work is often done outside school altogether, perhaps with a mentor who is not a teacher. There is a great deal of independence; the portfolio helps students by providing a structure and helps teachers keep track of each student's progress. At the same time, putting the portfolio online provides an appropriate level of accountability. Uploading the actual evidence enables teachers and administrators to gain insight into the student's work, as well as the struggles and triumphs that occurred along the way.

These various types of portfolios can be linked, as we will see in Chapter 2. To earn a badge, a student can submit both projects and individual classroom assignments; the evidence in the portfolio can contain both student-generated and teacher-generated entries. A project portfolio could well be a demonstration of the expectations listed in the "best work" portfolio. The variety of projects and assignments within a portfolio are limited only by the imagination of the students and teachers.

All these digital portfolio structures offer a way of organizing the contents so that the student work tells a story about the student's achievements. This structure not only helps the student decide what goes into the portfolio but also helps the audience—whether they're teachers, parents, or the students themselves—make connections among the various artifacts.

Why It's Worth It

Throughout the rest of this book, you will see how schools have successfully put badges and portfolios in place. But before starting on the details of *how* to work with portfolios, let's consider three reasons *why* it's worth the effort.

Promoting Personalization

When done well, digital portfolios and badges provide an opportunity for true personalized learning (DiMartino & Wolk, 2010; Kallick & Zmuda, 2017; Zmuda, Curtis, & Ullman, 2015). The portfolio, again, is a collection of work; the badges are a set of expectations to meet. Students could fill a portfolio with independent projects that show growth over time. The expectations behind the badges need not be limited to state requirements; students could define their own requirements as well. This process works well in both traditional and unconventional settings. Even in the most traditional schools, allowing a level of student voice in the process is crucial to students seeing the portfolio as something that represents something personal about themselves, instead of just another thing to do.

From a teacher's perspective, a digital portfolio provides a way of better understanding each student's strengths and weaknesses. When teachers see the badges of the class as a whole, the visual provides a quick sense of the class's current status. What areas do the students need to work on? Where have they already been successful? The portfolio also allows for a "deep dive" as needed. Moreover, patterns may surface in past work that may not have been obvious before. One student's portfolio could reveal, for example, a great ability to write fantastic stories but a reluctance to describe anything personal. Understanding the strengths and weaknesses of individuals, and of the class as a whole, enables the teacher to adjust the teaching according to each specific class's needs.

The digital portfolio has advantages for students across all ability levels. Some students may be looking for artifacts that show their successes; colleges are now beginning to incorporate digital portfolios (called *virtual lockers*) into the admissions process (Coalition for Access, Affordability, and Success, 2016). For other students who might struggle on traditional measures, the portfolio provides an alternative way to express their abilities. For example, evidence of a student's oral communication skills may be included to supplement his or her written skills, and the portfolio can be updated to show progress as often as needed.

Perhaps, however, this initiative particularly benefits the so-called average student. When students present their portfolios in end-of-year reviews or parent conferences, teachers often say, "I didn't know that about you!" Simply being able to talk to students about their overall reflections and what they consider to be their best work can provide a level of personalization that doesn't typically occur in regular classroom interactions.

Creating a Common Vision

Many schools go through the motions of establishing common expectations. Curriculum guides are printed; standards are posted at the front of the room. Digital badges, however, require that teachers and students come to a common understanding about what the expectations actually mean—and they have to define what work is going to be "good enough."

When students earn a badge online, they need to produce the evidence that led to that badge. Typically, the evidence comes from classroom assignments and projects. Thus, teachers need to provide *opportunities* to earn those badges. This means that the classroom assignments need to be linked to the school's expectations and, often, to common rubrics.

This is an opportunity for teachers to start looking at one another's assignments. Collectively, a set of teachers can share assignments and discuss which tasks will be most useful for their pool of students. In addition, teachers can review student work, and students need to feel assured that work that would earn a badge in one class will be honored in other classes. Chapter 4 will look at calibration exercises that help teachers align their assessments. Emphasizing a *common* vision means that teachers cannot feel they are doing this work in isolation; the portfolio provides a window into what's happening in other classes. In portfolio reviews, teachers need to engage with the collective understanding of what the expectations mean.

Similarly, students can no longer treat expectations in the abstract. They need to earn badges; to do this, they need to complete the requirements; to complete the requirements, they need to understand the expectations. As the process becomes more personalized, students will necessarily become more engaged with the expectations. It's not unusual for students to ask for opportunities to earn a badge: "What can I do to show my problem-solving skills?" The activity of collecting and assessing work creates a level of engagement with the school's expectations—for students, teachers, and parents.

Promoting Culture Change Through Conversation

It's easy for students and teachers to get lost in the modern curriculum. Many schools feel overwhelmed by the number of new things they're being asked to juggle: new standards, new curricula, new initiatives, new technologies. Everything feels like it's one more thing to add.

Badges and portfolios enable schools to focus. Typically, teachers will designate a few—two to four—key assignments for the portfolio. At the elementary level, this may involve looking at a couple of independent readings at different points of the year; at the secondary level, teachers may think about culminating assignments or projects. As a starting point, teachers can look at existing assignments.

Badges help schools implement the idea of planning backward (McDonald, 1992). Starting with the vision of what students should know and be able to do, teachers can designate the assignments and projects that will demonstrate those skills and knowledge. Students know these are opportunities to earn a portion of their badges; thus, teachers and students alike are looking at these performances a little more closely.

Because the student work is going into a portfolio—and may ultimately be used in the reviews or conferences—teachers and students know that this work may have value beyond the immediate grade in the classroom. We know from many years of research on authentic assessment (Darling-Hammond, 2014; Darling-Hammond, Ancess, & Falk, 1995; Wiggins, 1998) that an audience motivates students to focus a little more. Teachers feel similarly about the assignments included in the portfolio; it's a glimpse into their own classrooms. If colleagues are going to see the work, they would like to make sure that their assignments are portfolio-worthy.

For administrators looking to transform their schools, the badges are an opening for new conversations. Principals can go to department- or grade-level groups of teachers and simply ask, What assignments are you currently giving that will help students earn a badge? It sounds simple, but unpacking that question can get at the heart of the teaching process. More fine-tuned questions can follow: Which two or three assignments do you want to focus on? What is important about those assignments? What are students demonstrating? How do these assignments link to our school expectations? None of this needs to question the specific selection that the teachers make; rather, the conversation can help teachers clarify what's truly important for students to take away from their classes.

Badges are exciting to many educators for a variety of reasons. Michelle Riconscente, Amy Kamarinen, and Margaret Honey (2013) surveyed a variety of badge initiatives and found that "the appeal of badges is multifold" (p. 5) and that motivations include the following:

- Keeping up with "changing workforce demands."
- Providing incentives for "the acquisition of specialized skills."
- Overcoming "the shortcomings of standardized tests."
- Recognition that "learning experiences ... span various contexts."

I would also add that badges appeal to those who understand that many fields are rapidly changing; it's easy to add a new badge for a new programming language or a scientific skill that is just emerging.

Badges also acknowledge the changing landscape of education; "credits" are no longer limited to the classroom. As Sheryl Grant (2014) put it,

> The openness and portability of digital badges underpins how people learn anywhere, anytime, within and beyond traditional schools in a networked society. Until open digital badges emerged, learning happened anywhere, anytime, on multiple devices, in many contexts, but a standardized form of *recognition* did not. (p. 20)

Schools as institutions can provide the credibility and authority to place value on the badges.

The presentation of portfolios can be an opportunity to showcase best work—and reflect on progress. The online component of digital badges and portfolios means that students, teachers, and parents can engage with the student's progress at any time. There is also something to be said for a face-to-face conversation where the student is at the center. It's an opportunity to look beyond reading, math, or music in isolation; it's a chance—rare at the elementary level and almost nonexistent at the secondary level—for teachers and students to talk about their work as a whole. For students, the process of curating the work for presentation, including the reflection on what the work represents, is powerful; the idea that teachers and parents have set aside time to hear about each student's goals and progress can be life changing.

Matt Renwick (2017) describes an elementary school where students sit with teachers at multiple points—six times in all—through the year. He describes a 2nd grade student, Calleigh, sitting with her teacher, Janice, to discuss the student's writing. The teacher and student look together through a set of Calleigh's samples, and they begin to talk about her strengths. Calleigh is focused on her actual handwriting; she can see how her penmanship has improved from one piece to the next, and when asked what she wants to work on next, she says, "spacing." The teacher gently starts to discuss the actual content of the writing, praising her for her organization and explaining to Calleigh what organization actually means. Janice then is able to help Calleigh identify an area for improvement—to look at how she ends her essays. Through this conversation, Calleigh is able to reflect on her own work. As Janice guides her toward looking at the content as well as the handwriting, Calleigh can start to understand what makes a compelling piece of writing. Through such a process, schools can return, even just a bit, to being more student centered.

Schools that are successful in implementing portfolios start with a vision of what they want to achieve; the educational purpose needs to be clear to teachers and students, administrators, and parents. While the big picture provides the framework, the details are where schools make it happen. Let's look further at how we schools can define digital badges and their requirements in the next chapter.

Defining Badges

What do we want our students to know and be able to do?

This question is, simultaneously, the most mundane and the most profound question that schools can address. On the one hand, it's just a part of the daily routine. Every day's lessons start with "What are we going to do today?" Figuring out the activities is just a normal part of every teacher's prep work.

At the same time, each individual day is supposed to add up to something bigger—days become quarters, which become years, which become school careers. When we think about what we want students to know and do *overall*, we think differently than we do when considering what we want students to know and do *today*.

Digital badges and portfolios can help connect the short term and the long term. The badge is a visual representation of the long-term goal; as we shall see later in this chapter, a typical badge has multiple requirements and can't be completed in a single setting. But the badge is something students can see every day, whenever they log in; it serves as a reminder that today's activities are connected to something bigger.

Before beginning a school year with implementing badges, schools need to think about where they want students to be at the end of the year. Defining the set of badges will guide the work of students and teachers by defining the areas of focus. At the same time, it can illuminate possibilities by pointing to areas of study and inquiry that go beyond the traditional course catalog.

In this chapter, we will look at various types of badges. The subsequent chapters will delve deeper into the badge requirements and assessments.

Starting with the End in Mind

Imagine it's graduation day. As you think about your students walking across the stage to receive their diplomas, what is it that earned them their spot in line? (This exercise works even if you don't teach at a high school. What does it mean to complete middle school? Or to complete an elementary grade level?)

The most obvious answer is mechanical: The students passed the correct number of courses in the prescribed subject areas and therefore qualify to graduate. But what do "four years of English" or "three credits of science" actually represent? The curriculum guide will list lots of standards and units of study. Students should know about history, physics, and health; they should be able to write narratives, conduct experiments, and multiply fractions.

Culturally, though, graduation has a deeper meaning. It's a rite of passage; each year represents another level of maturity. (Walking through hallways, who hasn't heard the admonishments, "I wouldn't expect that from my 5th graders!" or "You're in middle school now; we expect more of you!"?) Current terminology says we want graduates to be college or career ready. Scratch the surface of those terms, and we understand this to mean that students are organized and independent, that we can rely on them to show up on time and persist.

Of course, all this is coming from the adults' perspective. What do students *themselves* want from school? For many, school is a means to an end; if the goal is to earn a spot at an elite university, school can be about building the credentials through classwork and extracurricular activities. If the goal is to achieve a certain level of financial security, then school is about getting practical skills. For some students, school is an opportunity to pursue a passion or explore something new and untried, be it academics, sports, or the arts. For students who may not be as focused, school is about getting through the day, the week, the year, and hoping they can pick up some skills and knowledge along the way.

So, when a school attempts to answer the question "What do we want our students to know and be able to do?" it is really trying to define its purpose. A diploma or an end-of-year certificate is a representation of what the school truly values.

The official graduation requirements for most schools usually read as a list of subject areas or skills: writing, reading, speaking, listening, mathematics, health education, performance in the arts. Many schools also have mission statements that list their aspirations for students. For example, in Rhode Island, Ponaganset High School's Core Values statement includes nine qualities it hopes to see in its students, including that students should become "effective communicators, independent researchers, reflective individuals, self-directed learners." In another city in the same state, Central Falls School District wants to help its "diverse student population" become "responsible citizens, effective communicators, innovative problem solvers, and critical thinkers who are able to fully participate in and positively contribute to society." In short, the requirements are lists of nouns and verbs; the mission statements emphasize the adjectives.

A badge system lets a school combine these nouns, verbs, and adjectives into a single set. Badges represent the *whole child* approach. This collection of skills, knowledge, and attributes is our aspirations for our students at all levels—and, when done well, they can show students paths for their own personal aspirations. If we think of badges as individual tiles, then each student's collection is his or her own mosaic of badges. Some will represent mastery of competencies, common across all students; others will be personalized by each student.

Here's another analogy. The late 19th century model of schooling, known as the *factory model*, assumed that student knowledge could be efficiently poured into a student as if we were creating an education on an assembly line—40 minutes of English followed by 40 minutes of science, and, at the end of the line, we have an educated person. A badge system *could* be placed on top of a factory model; at the end of each shift (or year), end-of-year grades can be translated into badges. One problem with the factory model, though, has always been the inconvenient fact that students do not all learn at the same pace (Sizer, 1992); another problem is that it assumes that all of the important information can be poured into students from curriculum guides (Wiggins, 1989).

Badges, on the other hand, allow a different approach; imagine students scattering all of the badges out on a table, like blocks or Lego bricks, and building their own structures. Some fundamental pieces are useful for any construction, but students may well take different combinations of them and work on them in their own order. Badges can allow for a deeply personalized approach to schooling—or, at a minimum, they can be a small step toward providing a little more personalization than schools offer now.

Elements of a Badge

A digital badge is a visual way of representing an accomplishment; simply put, it's a credential. More formally, "a digital badge represents a judgment by an organization or individual regarding a person's experiences, abilities, knowledge of qualifications" (Riconscente et al., 2013, p. 1).

Each badge definition contains the following elements:

Name

A badge's name should be clear to the student (and any other viewer). Avoid using acronyms that are unfamiliar to newcomers; you might know that "C&H" refers to "Culinary and Hospitality," but that may not be obvious to students or parents when they first walk in.

Scope

Is this badge something a student could earn after a unit of study? After a full course? After multiple years? (Some badges are called *micro-credentials* because they are smaller than a full credit, but you can define the scope of your badges however you like. Perhaps we should think of the badges that cut across multiple courses or years as *macro-credentials*.)

Requirements

To earn this badge, the student may need to complete a certain number of assignments, log some hours, demonstrate a skill, or do all of the above. The requirements should be concrete activities that the student can complete or behaviors that the student is likely to demonstrate during the natural rhythms of the school day. The requirements are the specific evidence that a student can produce to earn the badge.

Criteria

The criteria are what determines if a student actually earns a badge. These are assessment tools, such as rubrics, that are used to evaluate the student's evidence. To be fair to students (and ensure the badge system works across the school or throughout the district), the criteria need to be spelled out. One strategy is to create a common rubric to accompany the badge. For example, a student might earn a science badge by completing lab reports and earning a "proficient" mark on the common lab report rubric. Other criteria are also possible; what's most important is that the criteria are understandable and transparent.

Required/Elective

You can designate some of your badges as "required" by asking the question "Is a student required to earn this badge before going on to the next level or before graduation?" If a badge isn't required, it is considered an "elective" badge. Note that required badges can still include some student choice. For example, to earn an Arts badge, the student might choose among Music, Visual Arts, Dance, or Theater.

Levels/Prerequisites

You might divide badge requirements into a set of levels. For example, you might take a science badge and define gold, silver, and bronze levels. The bronze level is expected for all students (complete lab reports), whereas a gold level represents outstanding achievement (complete an independent inquiry). Some badges may be prerequisites for others; a badge in "advanced lifesaving skills" could require that the student has already earned a regular "lifesaving skills" badge.

Icon

The visual impact of badges cannot be underestimated. Badges are a visual representation of achievement and convey a great deal of information. In general, stick with simple designs; you will want to register the meaning of an icon with just a glance. Many good icons for badges are available online—or you can turn the creation of icons into a project for your students.

Badge Lists

Let's return to the original question, What do we want a graduate to know and be able to do? If you're a teacher, what are the most important things that a student should carry away from your classroom? If you hold a position outside the classroom, what are the crucial things that you think students should see across the board? As you make this list, it may be helpful to divide your list into the two columns of "academic/content" and "attitudes/behaviors," with the first column corresponding to the nouns and verbs and the second column corresponding to the adjectives.

Each individual—student, teacher, or administrator—may have his or her own list. Collectively, you might have dozens (or even hundreds) of items that you and your school community have suggested. What makes a badge system successful for a school is *combining* those individual lists into a coherent whole.

What follows are a number of lists used in different schools. The first three are academic badge lists; the remaining lists focus on habits and meta-cognitive skills. While these lists are useful as examples, it would be a mistake to simply adopt any other school's list outright. Often, what makes a list useful is the conversation within a school community when it creates its own list. In fact, the lists presented here are often second or third versions; the schools that created each list regularly reviews and revises its contents, based on its own community conversations and self-study. These lists are thus offered as starting points.

Academic Badges: Organized by Subject

To start, consider the set of high school graduation requirements shown in Figure 2.1. (Note that while this is from a high school, a very similar list could be made for middle or elementary school students.)

In the center column, this school has listed 24 badges, divided into nine categories. The first five categories have to do with various communications skills. We see badges for

- Listening (Requirement 1)
- Speaking (Requirement 2)
- Informational Writing (Requirements 3–6)
- Personal Writing (Requirements 7–9)
- Reading (Requirements 10–11)

To earn each badge, a student has to complete a certain number of proficient entries at some point during his or her high school career. Thus, to earn a speaking badge, the student needs one proficient entry; to earn the informational writing badge, the student needs six proficient entries. (We will get back to the idea of what makes something "proficient" in a moment.)

Note that the badge titles are deliberately broad. For example, requirement 3 simply says "Report Writing." This school did not want to tie all of

FIGURE 2.1 | **High School Badge Requirement List**

Badge	Graduation Portfolio Requirements	Number of Proficient Entries
	1. Listening Effectively (Interactive Listening)	1
	2. Speaking Effectively (Oral Presentations)	1
	3. Report Writing 4. Procedural Writing 5. Persuasive Writing 6. Text-Based Writing	6
	7. Reflective Writing 8. Narrative Writing 9. Poetry Writing	2
	10. Reading and Responding to an Informational Text 11. Reading and Responding to a Literary Text	3
	12. Problem Solving	4
	13. Numbers and Operations 14. Geometry and Measurement 15. Functions and Algebra 16. Data, Statistics, and Probability	6 (must include at least one of each)
	17. Think Sequentially 18. Investigate, Analyze, and Interpret Informational Resources	3
	19. Investigate Through Inquiry 20. Understand Systems and Energy 21. Relate Form to Function 22. Apply Scientific Principles to Real-World Situations	4
	23. Arts	Must earn a Visual Arts, Theater, or Music badge (as determined by those departments)
	24. Technology	Must build a digital portfolio

Source: Mt. Hope High School, Bristol-Warren Regional School District, Rhode Island. Used with permission.

the requirements—particularly those related to communication skills—to specific departments. The reports to complete the badge could be research papers from English, lab reports from science, or project reports from social studies. This list of requirements is set up so students see that they can complete this set, no matter what combination of courses they take.

Requirements 19–22 on the list (Investigate Through Inquiry, Understand Systems and Energy, Relate Form to Function, Apply Scientific Principles to Real-World Situations) are a little more specific than the communications skills, in that the students will most likely encounter these within science classes. However, they are broad within the scientific discipline; students can meet these requirements in earth science, biology, chemistry, physics, or any other science class.

This speaks to the broader point of creating the list of academic requirements. Rather than simply equating credits with seat time (four years of English, three years of science), this list gets at the fundamental skills that every graduate should possess. Most of these concepts will be addressed many times throughout a student's high school courses. This kind of list, with a small number of items in each category, shows the underpinnings of the curriculum.

Consider the requirements most closely connected to social studies (Requirements 17 and 18: Think Sequentially; and Investigate, Analyze, and Interpret Informational Resources). One can easily imagine a list of social studies requirements that enumerates all the important topics that students should know. (In fact, one doesn't even have to imagine. Lists like this have made up the bulk of many standards documents since, at least, the popularity of E.D. Hirsch's *Cultural Literacy* published back in 1987.) Instead, the focus is on two key skills that are at the heart of the discipline. The ability to "think sequentially" asks students to have a sense of what comes before, during, and after. Before we can have any conversation around cause and effect, we have to establish the sequence in which events occurred. Similarly, the skill of working with informational resources is crucial in all areas of social studies: Document-based questions in history, stock market charts in economics, or debate transcripts in civics all ask students to review sources of data and make a cogent analysis of what they mean. These two requirements—sequential thinking and analyzing information sources—are skills that any student should hone in any social studies class.

Now you may be thinking there are skills that you would add to this list, other things that you are completely convinced that every student should know and be able to do. And that's fine! This list of requirements is provided as a model, not as an absolute truth. What's important is that the badges represent a list of skills and knowledge that you can defend; you can make an argument for each and every requirement on the list as something all students should know and be able to do.

Note that this list focuses on skills more than content knowledge. Please do not take this to mean that content is unimportant; content, indeed, is crucial. Students at this school still spend plenty of time learning about right angles, the Renaissance, and ionic bonds. They take plenty of electives in world languages, business, and technology. This list of skills is *not* saying that content is unimportant; it *is* saying that students need to be able to *do* something with the content. We'll return to this idea in more depth later.

For the Arts requirement, students at this school have a choice: They can complete the Music badge, the Theater badge, or the Visual Arts badge. Each of these badges has its own independent requirements, which are roughly equivalent. Students can usually complete the badge with one or two of their courses. This introduces another element of choice into the badge system; although all students need to complete an Arts badge, there are multiple paths to earn one.

Finally, the school has a technology requirement: the digital portfolio itself. In the process of putting together entries that meet all of the other requirements, the school figures that students will gain the minimal set of technology skills expected of a graduate.

Let's look at the list in the right-hand column of the table for a moment; it's titled "Number of Proficient Entries." For each of the badges, students have to complete a certain number of entries. At this school, each class has multiple opportunities for students to add entries to the portfolio. That is, each teacher will typically select between three and six assignments (from a full-year class) and designate them as "portfolio-worthy." These assignments are tied to specific requirements; for example, a lab report might be connected to requirements 3 and 19. Generally speaking, the assignments are just like any other assignments from the class. The teacher sets the assignment, students turn it in, and then the teacher assesses the work. These assignments are part of the student's regular grades and get averaged into the usual end-of-quarter and end-of-year grade point averages (GPAs).

Two things separate these portfolio assignments from other assignments in the school. First, teachers have agreed to use common rubrics. Each of the requirements has its own rubric row; thus, any teacher in the school who is linking an assignment to requirement 3 is agreeing to use the schoolwide rubric for requirement 3. An assignment is considered "proficient" if the teacher gives it a proficient score on the schoolwide rubric (in this case, at least a "3" on a 4-point rubric).

Second, the assignments themselves have been vetted through a schoolwide committee process. In the first years of working with portfolios, this school had multiple sessions where faculty reviewed the assignments that could potentially be used in the digital portfolio. Using protocols (such as the tuning protocol described in Allen & Blythe, 2004; Easton, 2009; McDonald, Mohr, Dichter, & McDonald, 2013), the faculty looked at the proposed assignments. These assignments were usually already in place in the classes, but most of the time, they needed some tweaking to fit the schoolwide rubric. The faculty had to come to an agreement that these assignments would generate student work that was worthy of a badge.

Thus, the number of proficient entries listed on the requirements page represents just a small fraction of the total assignments students will encounter over four years. The student needs just one proficient speaking entry and six proficient informational writing entries. Still, these proficient entries, entered into the portfolio, can represent a great sampling of a student's high school career. Students will include work from multiple years and from most (if not all) departments.

At this school, about one-third of the students are able to complete all of the portfolio requirements by the end of 11th grade. (This doesn't mean they're automatically ready to graduate; students still need to complete a certain number of course credits as well.) The majority of the students need all four years to complete enough tasks at a proficient level.

Academic Badges: Organized by Skill

Let's consider another badge requirement list, as seen in Figure 2.2. This set of badges focuses on a broad set of skills. The definition for each of the expectations begins with "the process of," which implies that students are demonstrating something active. Many of the expectations ask the student to gain some knowledge ("understanding") and then use that knowledge in some way (such as "forming a critical stance" or "responding independently").

Even more than the first set of requirements we looked at, this list is separated from the academic disciplines. The skills of problem solving, communicating, or demonstrating innovative thinking can occur in any class. Now, the reality is that certain classes are more likely to have tasks associated with certain expectations. For example, there is typically more writing in the humanities classes than in the sciences. Still, the expectations are written for the school community as a whole, and faculty can use these as needed in any discipline.

FIGURE 2.2 | **Graduation Badge List**

	Expectation 1 **Problem Solving**	The process of effectively applying the analysis, synthesis, and evaluative processes in both independent and group settings to enable productive problem solving
	Expectation 2 **Communication:** **A. Interactive Communication**	The process of understanding, organizing/developing, speaking, listening/responding, and collaborating
	Expectation 2 **Communication:** **B. Reading**	The process of understanding, interpreting, connecting to, and forming a critical stance on textual material
	Expectation 2 **Communication:** **C. Writing**	The process of expressing ideas through writing in a variety of forms, using standard language conventions and considering various audiences
	Expectation 3 **Information, Media,** **and Technology Skills**	The process of ethically using a variety of 21st century tools to acquire and disseminate information, solve authentic problems, and increase productivity
	Expectation 4 **Innovative Thinking**	The process of demonstrating originality, creativity, flexibility, and adaptability in thinking patterns, work processes, and working/learning conditions
	Expectation 5 **Cultural/Civic Awareness** **and Personal Responsibility:** **A. Cultural Awareness**	The process of understanding diverse cultures, recognizing global relationships, and responding independently to changing conditions
	Expectation 5 **Cultural/Civic Awareness** **and Personal Responsibility:** **B. Civic Awareness**	The process of understanding social responsibility in relation to community
	Expectation 5 **Cultural/Civic Awareness** **and Personal Responsibility:** **C. Personal Responsibility**	The process of understanding personal accountability and its effects on quality of life

Source: Tourtellotte Memorial High School, North Grosvenordale, Connecticut. Used with permission.

Although these expectations are broad, there are ways that individual teachers or departments can make them a little more specific. Tourtellotte took the interesting approach of putting the specificity in the rubrics.

Consider these two rows from Expectation 5C, as shown in Figure 2.3.

FIGURE 2.3 | **Expectation Rubric**

Expectation 5C. Personal Responsibility				
Criteria	4 (Exemplary)	3 (Proficient)	2 (Needs Improvement)	1 (Unacceptable)
Application (Health)	Uses multiple reliable sources of health and wellness information to make thoughtful and appropriate health-related decisions	Uses reliable sources of health and wellness information to make appropriate health-related decisions	Uses some health and wellness information to make health-related decisions	Uses little to no health and wellness information to make health-related decisions
Application (Academic)	Defines, prioritizes, and completes tasks without direct oversight; sets and meets high standards and goals for delivering quality work on time	Defines, prioritizes, and completes tasks with little direct oversight; sets and meets adequate standards and goals for delivering work on time	Defines, prioritizes, and completes tasks with some direct oversight; sets and meets some standards and goals for delivering work on time	Defines, prioritizes, and completes tasks with continuous direct oversight; sets and meets low standards and goals for delivering work on time

Source: Tourtellotte Memorial High School, North Grosvenordale, Connecticut. Used with permission.

When a teacher decides that a task is a good demonstration of the expectation of "personal responsibility," he or she can decide on which rows of the rubric to use. The row related to health asks students to make informed decisions about their well-being; the row related to academics asks students to work independently and deliver on time. Both are reasonable demonstrations of "personal responsibility," and teachers can thus make an appropriate determination of which rubric is most appropriate for the specific entry.

As schools become more personalized, these broad statements can serve the school well. Students can create their own expectations or submit work from outside experiences (from dual-enrollment classes to online courses). It can then be up to the student to determine which badge is being addressed by a particular entry; the broad statements, such as those in Figure 2.3, allow the school to accept a broader set of possible entries.

Academic Badges: Organized by Modes of Thought

Another approach to defining academic badges is to focus on modes of thought. For example, the International Baccalaureate (2017) bases its Primary Years Programme around six transdisciplinary themes. These areas of inquiry include the following:

- Who we are
- Where we are in time and place
- How we express ourselves
- How the world works
- How we organize ourselves
- Sharing the planet

At the same time, the program has expectations in six subject areas:

- Language
- Social studies
- Mathematics
- Arts
- Science
- Physical, social, and personal education

In a digital badge system, students could earn badges in each of these 12 areas. A project will typically overlap the two lists; it could easily connect to a "sharing the planet" area of inquiry while also demonstrating a student's skills in language or science. Thus, these two sets represent different views of the curriculum and may provide some insight into a student's specific strengths. A student may put up average grades as a matter of calculating an end-of-year score, but in looking at the items submitted for the portfolio, it becomes apparent that the student demonstrates stronger performances in tasks related to "how we express ourselves" compared to, say, "how we organize ourselves." It might be that one particular unit or area of study is of greater interest to the student; perhaps the student is perfectly fine with studying science or art but has less interest in the specific assignment for this year's work.

Badges for Habits of Mind

It's tempting, when thinking about badge lists, to focus on the final products that students will create. However, if a school wants its badges to represent the whole child, the school's list needs to allow students to demonstrate their habits and dispositions.

One powerful method is for a school to organize badges around the "habits of mind." As Costa and Kallick (2008) put it in their seminal work:

> Educational outcomes in traditional settings focus on how many answers a student knows. When we teach for the Habits of Mind, we are interested also in how students behave when they *don't* know an answer. (p. 16)

The habits of mind help students contribute to their ability to be continual learners (Costa & Kallick, 2008):

- Persisting
- Managing impulsivity
- Listening with understanding and empathy
- Thinking flexibly
- Thinking about your thinking
- Striving for accuracy
- Questioning and problem posing
- Applying past knowledge to new situations
- Thinking and communicating with clarity and precision
- Gathering data through all the senses
- Creating, imagining, and innovating
- Responding with wonderment and awe
- Taking responsible risks
- Finding humor
- Thinking interdependently
- Remaining open to continuous learning

Each of these habits can correspond to a badge. Will a student demonstrate all 16 of these? Maybe, over time. As you think about your classes, you may see some habits more often than others; "striving for accuracy" may be more common than "responding with wonderment and awe." As a school, you may decide it isn't crucial for students to receive a badge in every single one of these habits; the point of using badges is to enable students to show what strategies they use to become better thinkers. The badges help students identify which habits they use most regularly (and, by extension, which habits they would like to practice more).

The habits of mind badges (along with the remaining badge lists in this chapter) can be used in conjunction with the academic badges listed previously. The habits are defined as "characteristics of what intelligent people do when they are confronted with problems" (Costa & Kallick, 2008, p. 15). When a student is working on an entry for a writing badge or a science badge and is confronted with a problem, how did the student handle it? It's very likely that the entry the student submits for the academic badge could also be a demonstration of one of the habits of mind. So, when students are adding entries, they can be encouraged to reflect on what problems they encountered and what strategy they used to resolve it. This reflection can then be the evidence needed to earn the habits badge; the same piece of work can demonstrate both academic mastery and a habit of mind.

Badges for Work Habits and Success Skills

Badges can also be awarded for demonstrating certain behaviors. We can characterize these as *work habits* or *success indicators*. Many such lists exist in the world; one elegant list comes from the Ontario Ministry of Education's *Growing Success* report (2010). Students in all grades need to demonstrate

- Responsibility
- Organization
- Independent work
- Collaboration
- Initiative
- Self-regulation (the ability to set goals, make plans, and persevere)

Each of these areas is accompanied by a list of sample behaviors. For example, "organization" includes the following samples:

The student:

- Devises and follows a plan and process for completing work and tasks.
- Establishes priorities and manages time to complete tasks and achieve goals.
- Identifies, gathers, evaluates, and uses information, technology, and resources to complete tasks. (Ontario Ministry of Education, p. 11)

Because this list of work habits was meant to be used for all grade levels, the specific demonstrations of "devises and follows a plan" should be age appropriate. Presumably, older students should be able to devise and follow more complex plans than younger ones.

Additionally, this list of behaviors is not meant to be all-encompassing; there are many other ways that students can show they're organized. For example, a middle school student who takes responsibility for walking his or her younger siblings to school each day or takes on other family obligations may be showing a great deal of organizational skill. Still, this list provides a template for students and teachers; it not only articulates the work habits that are useful in the world outside school but also describes how students can show those behaviors within the elementary, middle, or high school environment.

Another list of success skills was articulated by Thomas R. Hoerr (2017) as "the formative five":

- Empathy
- Self-control
- Integrity
- Embracing diversity
- Grit

The formative five are the "skills necessary for success in both the work world and relationships of all kinds" (p. 9). Like the other skills we've seen, the formative five can be demonstrated by students throughout their years in school at age-appropriate levels. One of Hoerr's most important observations is that "significantly and encouragingly, *the Formative Five skills are teachable*, regardless of the students' ages" (p. 11). With the academic badges, the assumption is that students will respond to a specific prompt (such as an assignment or a project) to demonstrate mastery. Success skills can work the same way; rather than just waiting for students to demonstrate empathy or self-control, teachers and advisors can specifically note when the opportunities arise. For example, when students are working on a group project, students can be told that this is a chance to demonstrate elements of the formative five.

Tony Wagner (2008) identified seven survival skills that students need to demonstrate to be successful in today's career environment:

- Critical thinking and problem solving
- Collaboration across networks and leading by influence
- Agility and adaptability
- Initiative and entrepreneurialism
- Effective oral and written communication
- Accessing and analyzing information
- Curiosity and imagination

A few of the seven survival skills (problem solving, communicating, analyzing information) could also count as academic goals, but demonstrating "curiosity" or "adaptability" isn't usually in any one department's curriculum guide.

The "work habits" category is where schools identify the attributes they expect of all students, but these typically do not show up on report cards beyond the primary years. Nevertheless, many schools include these ideas in their mission statements; certainly, most educators say they want students who are independent, who take initiative, and who are responsible.

By creating badges around these work habits and success skills, schools are saying that we should take these habits seriously. The work habits badges tell the school community two things. First, they indicate that the school will *teach* these things. Any educator will tell you that students entering school do not all immediately possess these skills. If we want all students to be able to collaborate or be organized, the school needs to provide opportunities for the students to learn how to do so. We should not simply assume that students will naturally pick up these skills. Ask any athletic coach or theater director about having students learn how to work together, and they will tell you about the techniques and teachable moments that turn a random group of individuals into a team. If a school is true to its mission, then those opportunities should be available for all students.

Second, work habits badges indicate that there is a *certain level of achievement* that the school expects of all students. What is a reasonable demonstration of collaboration? Is it enough for students to just show up at all the meetings, even if the student does not participate? Does the student have to show some kind of give-and-take with another member of the group?

Third, work habits badges can show that a student is ready for new challenges. A school might say that students who demonstrate mastery of certain work habits will be eligible for apprenticeship programs or other leadership roles. Earning badges, then, can be a concrete way of opening new opportunities for students.

How does a student earn a habits badge? Often, the work habits (and similarly, the habits of mind) may be simply something that the teacher observes. When a teacher sees something occur—in the classroom, in an after-school activity, in the halls, or online—that may be a moment to note, and that note could be used toward achieving a badge.

One school we've worked with uses a "flags" system. Teachers can write a note anytime online. (It's similar to a social media messaging system but is completely private within the school community of staff, students, and parents.) The teacher's note can be accompanied by a green, yellow, or red flag; green flags signal encouraging activities, whereas red flags signal items that require a closer look. For example, a teacher might create a note with a red flag if a student is regularly submitting work late, while a teacher could create a note with a green flag when a shy student is more willing to share thoughts during class discussions. These flags are individual observations; over time, students, parents, and teachers can see the set of flags; the accumulation of enough green flags could potentially be the evidence used to indicate that a student has earned a badge.

Of course, one can also use rubrics for the work habits badges. Anyone who has spent any significant time around students will be able to identify moments where students showed initiative or adaptability. For example, how does a student handle a situation where she is all set to present to the class—and the fire alarm goes off? When we collectively recall those moments, we can see some common elements, and those can be the basis of a rubric. Thus, when the teacher assesses the presentation, the teacher can note on the digital badge system that the student demonstrated the habit of "self-control."

Badges for Personal Interests

As schools move toward personalization, students should have more opportunities to pursue their particular interests and passions. Although we have discussed many badges thus far, no school has a totally comprehensive list of all the areas that students may want to pursue. Therefore, it's a good idea for schools to have a mechanism to enable students to create personal badges.

One way to start with personal badges is to ask students to create an *individual learning plan*. Students start their learning plan by setting goals: What are the students' long-term plans for college or career? What goal would they like to achieve in their academic work this year—or beyond? Are there personal or social goals that they want to achieve?

Part of the personal goal setting may be asking students to consider options that the school already has in place. For example, many schools are offering *pathways*, sequences of classes and opportunities to pursue certain fields in depth. Although pathways have long been in place in career and technical schools, many other schools are adding pathways as well, in everything from robotics to music production to health care.

A pathway badge can certainly overlap with other categories; clearly, demonstrating mastery of science is a crucial component of healthcare careers. It could be that the requirements for a pathway badge come from combining existing academic badges with a single project related to the field. For example, a student could earn a business badge by completing certain badges in math, communications, and civics and then participating in a project such as those sponsored by DECA or SkillsUSA. Here, the badge indicates that the student has demonstrated an interest in a particular field and has put in some time and effort to pursue that interest in concrete ways.

Figure 2.4 shows the connections between the goals, pathways, and badges. Here, the school has multiple pathways, such as Animal/Plant Science, Biomedical, and Computer Science. Within each pathway, there are multiple goals; in Figure 2.4, we see that the Computer Science pathway contains badges in Programming, Robotics, and Web Design. When the students create a goal, they can also select a corresponding badge. When they do, those badges appear on the student's list (as shown in the bottom row of Figure 1.1 on p. 8).

Turning this goal-setting exercise into badges creates a different level of commitment for the students. Traditionally, goal setting has simply been a once-a-year exercise that guidance counselors or advisors review when necessary. Instead, representing the student goal as a badge—and having a visual reminder every time the student logs in—announces that the student has an interest that he or she wants to pursue. It's the direct opposite of the "out of sight, out of mind" approach; seeing the badge helps keep the goal in mind. I'll return to individual learning plans in Chapter 6.

FIGURE 2.4 | **Pathway Badge**

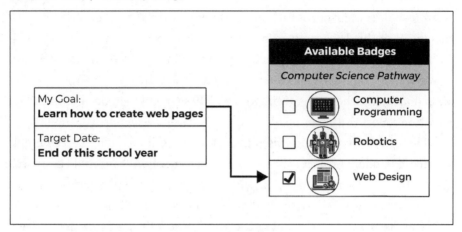

The list of goals is by no means limited to pathways; extracurricular offerings from sports and clubs, as well as partnership offerings (such as activities sponsored by libraries or community organizations), can be included in the personal badges.

The requirements for these badges, including those in the pathways, may be defined by the school. The traditional comprehensive high school may have many offerings for students; seeing them listed in this format can give students a sense of their options and of the opportunities they can pursue while in school.

Although it's definitely useful for schools to show the badges that are already defined by existing offerings, there are undoubtedly students who want to pursue something that isn't listed. These are truly student-generated badges. A student-generated badge needs to contain the same elements as any other badge. Specifically, there should be requirements and criteria. For example, a student might propose a badge around gardening. Working with faculty, a student could think about the requirements, asking questions such as these:

- What background knowledge will be important?
- What skills do I need to demonstrate?
- What evidence can I produce?

In the gardening example, students can learn about what plants will be most useful in their corner of the world and when they are most likely to bloom. With this background knowledge, the student can make a proposal: to create a garden with these specific plants, taking up X amount of space and growing over the next Y weeks. With the teacher, the student can agree on what documents the student will produce; these might include anything from a written report to a time-lapse movie of the garden growing over time.

The criteria may rely on existing rubrics; your school might have common rubrics for student projects or aspects of problem solving that could be appropriate. There's also nothing wrong with students proposing the criteria themselves and having teachers verify that the criteria make sense for the project. As I will discuss in more detail in Chapter 4, you will want to watch for two common student errors: equating effort with success and assuming a positive outcome. In the case of the garden example, success should not equate to the garden yielding many plants.

Personal badges can be an entryway for your school to truly engage in personalized learning. They're an opportunity to engage in the framework for personalization suggested by Kallick and Zmuda (2017). A personal badge should allow for student voice, co-creation of criteria, a level of social construction, and an opportunity for self-discovery.

Personal badges do not have to be reinvented each time; the next student interested in gardening can adopt and adapt the badge created by a previous student. It's also certainly possible for these badges to become part of the regular curriculum. Consider how technology classes have evolved over time. In many schools, robotics was initially an after-school activity, but now it has become part of the technology curriculum. In fact, in some schools, it has become the required computer technology course for all students. Thus, it's clearly useful to make these personal badges accessible to other students.

Badges for College and Career Readiness

The idea of college and career readiness is very much an active issue for schools; for many students (and indeed, many adults), the whole purpose of school is to prepare students so they can earn a living (or go to college and then earn a living). The economic incentive certainly provides the motivation for many students to stay in school.

College- and career-readiness badges can provide practical milestones that show students are on their way to achieving their goals. Of course, many of the badges discussed thus far are part of any college or career preparation: An academic foundation, work habits, and personal interests all feed into a well-prepared student. There may also be specific things that we want to demonstrate in these areas.

Career badges have been around for a long time and have typically taken the form of certification. Many professions have a required set of skills, and many schools have incorporated those skills into their curricula. Some of these are regulated at the state level (such as cosmetology), whereas others are defined by industry (computer networking or automotive technologies). The requirements for a career badge can correspond directly to existing license or certificate programs.

Badges for college readiness overlap many of the categories I have discussed so far. Creating a demonstration of best work has gained new currency; starting in the 2016–17 school year, members of the Coalition for Access, Affordability, and Success started offering a new process for college admissions. The member schools of the coalition include more than 140 of the most prestigious colleges and universities in the United States. Its roster includes seven of the Ivy League universities; elite private universities across the country, from Duke, to the University of Chicago, to Stanford and CalTech; well-known smaller colleges, from Amherst to Pomona; and the majority of flagship state universities, such as the universities of Florida, Maryland, Michigan, and Washington. All of these colleges are looking to understand their applicants in new ways.

Using the Coalition's online tools, students can create a *virtual locker*. This can contain any work of the student's choosing from in or out of school, from a formal classroom or personal interest. In this way, students can essentially create a digital portfolio to use as a component for the college application process.

The specifics for what to submit depend on the particular university and field. For many years, students applying in the fields of art, music, or architecture were asked to submit examples of their work or performances, and as students have become more tech-savvy, colleges have allowed them to submit a video in lieu of one of the application essays or include a link to a research or independent project.

High school students, then, could work on a College Readiness badge that will prepare them for this new application process. Here are some of the questions that such a badge should answer:

- Can the student work independently?
- Does the student have strong communication skills?
- Does the student understand what is required for this major?
- Does the student have the tenacity to complete a four-year degree?

A badge corresponding to these questions could be useful to help students understand what strengths they bring to a college.

If your school regularly sends students to certain colleges, it's worth looking at what kinds of questions those colleges ask; a school district in Maryland, for example, would be wise to consider what questions are on the Coalition application for the University of Maryland. Of course, not all students will go to that one college, but as a starting point, examining the types of questions that the college wants students to answer will help indicate the type of information that the admissions staff finds useful. Thus, it makes sense that one requirement of the college readiness badge would be to consider how the student will answer the essay questions on a college application.

While these new developments in career and college readiness are exciting, they are still in relatively early stages. Employers, admissions officers, and placement personnel are also learning about how to best "read" the badges they receive. As such, it can help to focus your schools' college and career readiness badges on allowing students to show evidence that would not necessarily appear elsewhere. For example, in a workshop on "Micro-Credentials as Evidence for College Readiness," college admissions officers mentioned that they would like to see examples of students showing "sustained and deep engagement in a particular area," as opposed to "collecting activities for the purpose of 'résumé-polishing'" (Fishman, Teasley, & Cederquist, 2018, p. 16). As the popularity of badges increases, it's worth keeping an open conversation with your local employers, colleges, and trade schools to discuss what evidence they would most like to see from students that they don't currently see now.

How to Organize Badge Lists

As an exercise, your school could start by examining all of the categories we have discussed thus far and asking which badges you want to offer. What should quickly become apparent is that a school can provide many opportunities for badges; the list of possibilities can get very long.

Now the focus is on deciding which badges need to be *required*. That is, what does *every* student need to learn? Put another way, if it's graduation day and students are walking across the stage, what do you want to guarantee that each graduate can demonstrate? When we speak of a requirement, we're not talking about things that would be nice for all students to have. We're talking about badges that a failure to fulfill at an acceptable level result in a failure to graduate. For example, many schools want students to study a second language. But few schools require all students complete a certain level of proficiency in a second language in order to graduate.

The discussion of what badges should be required should engage the entire school community. The school is taking a stand; this is what it believes is a minimum set of skills for any graduate. Establishing a baseline set of badges provides a focus for the work of teachers and students throughout the school.

Remember, required badges can still be flexible. Students could earn a required arts badge by completing badges in music, theater, or visual arts. You might decide that all students need to complete a pathway badge—and then offer multiple choices. You could stipulate that students need to create at least one personal badge by designing an independent project.

At the same time, a badge system can show the breadth of options available to students. The badges that are not required can be labeled as "optional" or "elective." Many of these will stem from classes or activities already in place at the school. On the academic side, you may have badges that correspond to the subject areas or classes that already exist in your course catalog. Athletic teams, extracurricular clubs and activities, and community service projects all can be places where students earn badges. You may already have the requirements defined; the requirements for earning a varsity letter or a name in a concert program can translate into a badge.

Examples of required badge lists and optional badge possibilities are listed in the Appendix. Generally speaking, you probably don't want more than about 10 required badges. (These 10 could be broken down into various components.) It's helpful to have a list that is short enough that students and teachers can name them all off the top of their heads.

Setting Levels

Schools find it helpful to define levels for badges (such as gold, silver, bronze). After you've established where you want all students to be at the end, you can establish some reasonable milestones along the way. Allowing students to see a level of achievement even prior to the graduation level can be quite useful. You may also establish some additional levels to show a top level of achievement. For example, students showing exceptional skills in the arts could earn a special arts badge acknowledging that they have gone above and beyond.

Putnam High School, in Putnam, Connecticut, established the set of badges for graduation displayed in Figure 2.5.

For most of the expectations in this list, students need to earn a badge each year in each category; thus, the portfolio contains examples of "reading actively" in grades 9, 10, 11, and 12. A student entry that is good enough to earn a grade 9 badge may not be good enough to earn a grade 12 badge. Still, the level acknowledges the student's very real achievement in earning that grade 9 badge. It also reflects the student's current ability. The grade 12 badge is expected for graduation, whereas the grade 9 badge is not.

In this way, a badge system counteracts some of the false equivalencies that are built into schools. For example, a 9th grade English class may be worth the same number of credits as an advanced 12th grade class in British literature, but they require different levels of accomplishment. A visual demonstration in the form of a badge can provide the recognition that the 12th grader has achieved this more advanced gold level of achievement.

Another strategy for setting levels is called *goal attainment scaling*. Essentially, a student sets a goal for the end of the year. Working with a teacher, counselor, or special education advisor, the student's goal is divided into milestones. Lee Ann Jung (2018) describes how these milestones could be set monthly; if there are nine months in the school year, then we can divide the goal into nine monthly milestones. For example, if the student is going to work on demonstrating the competency of "analysis and synthesis of information," the student's goal for the first month is to identify sources of information; for the second month, it's to determine which sources are credible and why; by the sixth month, the milestone is to do a "compare and contrast" of different sources. In a badge system, these milestones could be represented as different color badges.

Each of the examples of badge lists in this chapter is an attempt to answer the question we started the chapter with: What do we want our students to know and be able to do? Creating a vision of a graduate—and being able to share that vision across the school community—gives the badge system its power.

FIGURE 2.5 | **Learner Expectations**

Academic Learning Expectations		
	1. Read actively	For each expectation • Students will include one completed entry (with summary, artifact, and reflection) for each grade level (9, 10, 11, 12). • Each entry must be assessed on a schoolwide rubric and be approved by a teacher.
	2A. Written communication	
	2B. Oral communication	
	3. Individual work	
	4. Group work	
	5. Problem solving	
	6. Using technology	
Civic and Social Expectations		
	7. Demonstrates personal and civic responsibility	Students must • Earn a physical fitness badge and • Earn a badge in "Understanding Responsibilities" or "School Community Involvement."
	8. Makes positive contributions within the school and community	Students must • Complete 20 hours of community service, maintained in a log.
	9. Respects, promotes, and celebrates diversity	Students must • Satisfy the expectation through school community involvement or demonstrate understanding of diversity through academics (one over four years) and • Demonstrate understanding of diversity through the arts (one over four years).

Source: Putnam High School, Putnam, Connecticut. Used with permission.

Earning Badges

A school's badge list is a vision of what a student should master. From there, the school has to establish the requirements for each badge. Most of the time, badges can be earned by completing classroom assignments. For example, we saw earlier that a student can earn an Informational Writing badge by producing reports and samples of procedural, persuasive, and text-based writing. The same entry may also be a demonstration of a habit of mind or success skill.

To make the system fair, students need to have opportunities to fulfill the requirements. It wouldn't be right to expect students to earn a badge for collaboration—and then not offer any opportunities for students to work together in groups. Increasingly, opportunities are no longer limited to the classroom; many schools have a community service requirement that is typically completed off school grounds. Still, there needs to be a way for students to get some mentoring and assistance in completing such a task. As you define the requirements for your badges, consider how each student is going to be able to complete them—and how you will handle it for students who have difficulty. We will spend more time on the types of tasks that students can complete in the next chapter.

3

Creating Portfolio-Worthy Tasks

How do students earn the badges?

What goes into the portfolio?

How do we create portfolio-worthy tasks?

One spring, at a high school in a southern suburban school district, a group of students were showing me their digital portfolios. This was back in the 1990s, and these students were participants in the very first research project on digital portfolios. Their initial prompt was simply to collect their best work from each of their classes and add some reflections. This small group of students shared many of the same classes, and some of the entries in their portfolios were quite impressive. There was a project from social studies in which the students developed ideas for a real-world issue—how to attract more visitors to the area's waterfront. There was a math project in which the students examined the geometry of stained glass windows. There were entries from Mr. Horan's computer technologies class, where students were learning about the latest hardware and software applications.

I noticed that one area was missing. I asked, "What about science?" The students responded, "Oh, we don't do anything in science." Then they talked about the class. They described how they answered questions at the end of each chapter and had a series of multiple-choice/fill-in-the-blank tests. Their lab experiments sounded more like rote demonstrations. As one student put it, "Is it really an experiment if you know what's going to happen ahead of time?"

The students had been told that their portfolios were to hold their best work: the work they would be proud to show to someone else. But the assignments and tests from their science class were not items these students wanted to show. In essence, they were saying that the tasks from this class were not "portfolio-worthy."

From Concept to Practice

After deciding on the list of badges, schools will naturally have a follow-up question: What do students need to do to earn the badges? Most teachers, when asked this question, will want to respond, "Here are the requirements. It's a list of things you can do to demonstrate that you have the skills that we expect of a student in grade X. And it's my job to help you achieve those requirements."

Tasks, or assignments, are where badges and portfolios stop being an abstract concept and start becoming a real classroom practice. As part of their daily activities, teachers can indicate how the work in each day's class is helping students move toward earning a badge. It's more motivating for students to see that today's assignment contains steps toward earning a gold badge than for them to understand that the lesson incorporates a set of standards listed in the front of the classroom. By linking lessons and tasks to the badges, teachers can keep students on track daily.

Badges gain their credibility from the evidence behind them. This evidence should show that the student has met the requirements and that the requirements are reasonable. Students, teachers, and other reviewers all need to be convinced by the submitted evidence. This means that the tasks that are connected to the badge need to be portfolio-worthy.

The good news is that there are a wide range of tasks that can be portfolio-worthy. Tasks can vary from on-demand assignments completed in a single class period to year-long projects that require multiple milestones. Tasks can be generated by teachers, students, or (if both agree) outside groups. For the majority of teachers, these tasks already exist and are currently part of your curriculum.

Generally speaking, a portfolio-worthy task

• Requires effort.

• Allows for some level of student voice and choice.

• Is authentic to the subject area.

- Requires an application of knowledge.
- Generates products that students would be proud to display.

In this chapter, we'll look at a variety of tasks, including *classroom tasks*, *projects and quests*, and *student-initiated tasks*, and discuss how to determine which ones are portfolio-worthy.

Classroom Tasks

The most common way that students earn badges is by completing classroom assignments. When a student completes an assignment and the teacher marks it as proficient, the assignment counts toward the badge. To earn a science badge, one requirement might be to have three proficient lab reports; to earn a creative writing badge, a student might need two proficient samples of fiction or poetry.

This doesn't mean, however, that *every* assignment has to go into the portfolio. Typically, students can add two to four entries for each full year class. At the elementary level, this might translate to two or three samples in reading and two or three from math.

The easiest way to get started is to designate certain assignments as *portfolio assignments*. This may be a specific assignment that all students will submit or one that students might select. A portfolio-worthy assignment is not going to be a math drill or a spelling test. Most likely, the tasks are those that demonstrate "strategic thinking" or "complex reasoning" (levels 3 or 4 on the Depth of Knowledge scale [Webb, 2002]). The portfolio-worthy task will be one that demonstrates the student's proficiency in the subject matter and fulfills the badge requirements.

It's easiest for teachers to start with tasks they already assign. When introducing digital portfolios and badges, there are often new things to ponder, from using the technical platform to thinking about student growth in new ways. By using existing tasks, teachers can feel more grounded in their work as they explore these new ideas.

At the same time, a badge initiative is also an opportunity to modernize the assessments and give them a more contemporary twist. In their book *Bold Moves for Schools: How We Create Remarkable Learning Environments* (2017), Heidi Hayes Jacobs and Marie Alcock distinguish among *classical*, *antiquated*, and *contemporary* assessments. Instead of a standard oral presentation, how about asking students to do a podcast, which could provide more opportunities for student voice? Are there types of collaboration—with other students in the class or with mentors who students could connect with online—that might be useful? Could we extend the idea of primary sources to include interviews with members of the community? School leaders need to find a balance between pushing for new ideas while ensuring that faculty aren't overwhelmed with too many new ideas simultaneously.

One way to get started is to set up a professional development session and go over the badge list your school has created. The ultimate goal is to establish the requirements for each badge on this list; to do this, though, it helps to identify possible tasks and projects that students are completing in their classes now. That means, in the current session, teachers will create a list using the form shown in Figure 3.1.

FIGURE 3.1 | **What Will Go into a Course Portfolio?**

Teacher: _____   **Course:** _____

Assignment	Badge	Date	Artifacts
Provide the title of an assignment you give in your course.	List the badges being assessed.	List the month you typically give this assignment.	List the artifacts that the student will enter into the portfolio (e.g., rough/final drafts, presentations, artwork).

When you ask your faculty to identify the tasks that will be used in the portfolio, you can provide this guide to think about the kinds of tasks that could be included:

- On-demand versus extended
- Growth over time (e.g., an oral presentation at the beginning of the year compared to one at the end of the year)
- Projects or quests
- Logs
- Incidental tasks
- Demonstrations of cross-cutting concepts/practices
- Cornerstone tasks
- Observations
- Student-initiated tasks

Acknowledging that there are different types of tasks can help open up teachers' imaginations. Faculty can think about how their tasks vary over the year; tasks have different lengths and require varying amounts of structure or preparation. Some tasks are teacher-driven, some student-initiated, and some require collaboration. Tasks can be designed to encourage student voice and choice.

As your faculty think about the tasks they think should be requirements, it helps to consider some examples. Let's look at possibilities from different subject areas.

Tasks in Writing

Writing portfolios have been around for a long time. In schools, the most common method is to have students include a sample of each genre: narrative, argumentative, reflective, research, and creative (including fiction or poetry). Writing, however, is as much about the process as the final product. One strategy, then, is to ask students to include at least one sample that contains all of the steps: initial idea, outline, graphic organizer, first draft, and final draft. This way, the reader of the portfolio can see the student's process from beginning to end, and the student can reflect on how he or she molded the initial idea into an entire essay.

At the elementary level, some schools make a list of common writing assessments; for example, in the fall of grade 2, students might be asked to write their own fairy tales. These common assessments can be useful in the portfolio by providing a baseline. Not *every* item in the writing portfolio needs to be from the list of common assessments, but it can be helpful to know that you'll see some common entries.

This may be a good time to distinguish between *on-demand* and *extended* tasks. On-demand tasks are typically done in class, like the traditional timed essay, but they can include any task where the student is expected to perform on the spot. On-demand tasks are not limited to writing; they can include theater performances, athletic events, or even standing before a group to answer questions. Extended tasks are done over a longer period of time and go beyond the classroom, such as a story a student writes at home or a research paper a student prepares over several weeks.

Both on-demand and extended tasks can be used to earn badges; the specific requirements are up to you as a school. Very often, the requirements for a course-level or graduation badge will include some tasks to demonstrate foundational skills and an extended task or project to show the application and synthesis of those skills. It's worth noting that not every task needs to be an extended, long-term project.

Tasks in Reading

For younger students, the reading tasks can be video clips of the student reading, as shown in Figure 3.2.

At this particular school, parent-teacher conferences take place twice a year, roughly at the end of the first and third quarters. Just before each conference, the students are filmed doing an independent reading.

In the portfolio, we see several things. First, we have the video of the student reading. Next, we see the text she's reading so we can follow along. Below that, we see links to a rubric and the teacher's narrative comments. The videos aren't very long, typically a minute or less. Still, they are powerful glimpses of a student's abilities.

Adding these other elements puts the video in context. We can see the difficulty of the text that the student is reading, as well as the comments from the teacher indicating her overall progress. The clip provides enough information that a reader (such as a parent or next year's teacher) can make sense of what the work represents.

Each reading entry becomes a point of context for the next entry. That is, when we look at a student's reading sample from the spring, we can compare it to the entry from the previous fall. In reading, it's not just about reaching a certain level of badge; it's also interesting to note the *growth over time*. The progress that the student makes from one conference to the next can be quite dramatic, especially in these early years when the students are first learning how to read. We can see them move from struggling just to decode the words on the page to confident readers who are able to read passages with full comprehension.

FIGURE 3.2 | **Elementary Reading Task**

	RICHER PICTURE®
Fall / Grade 1 🖉	
Entry Date	October 27
See me read	Download video 1 (original format) ▶ [━━━━━━━━━━] 00:10/04:34 ◻
Text of my reading	Don got up. The dog got up. Don and the dog went walking. Jan got up. The cat got up. Jan and the cat went walking.
Teacher Comments	Carlene is quiet and does not like to make a mistake. She is unsure of certain new words and needs encouragement, but is definitely making progress. She is eager to read and excited with each new success. (I believe the video camera made her appear less confident than usual). Continued practive with sight words and short vowel sounds will be helpful.
Rubric	Reading Rubric 🖉

Source: Copyright © 2018 Ideas Consulting, Inc. Used with permission.

As students move on through the years, from upper elementary into middle and high school, the reading samples will inevitably change. The focus is no longer on the mechanics of reading, but rather on comprehending, responding to the texts, and demonstrating a range of reading interests.

Various reading tasks can be designated as portfolio-worthy, including

- Group discussions about a particular reading.
- Response to literature essays.
- More contemporary tasks, such as creating skits, blogs, or animations. For example, at one high school, students created animations to illustrate classic literature, such as a stick-figure animation illustrating Edgar Allan Poe's *The Tell-Tale Heart*. Through this medium, the student demonstrated an understanding of the major plot elements, while also showing his own communication skills.

One strategy for building a reading badge is to have students complete a *reading log*. The log can contain a list that indicates what books or articles the students have read and when they read them. The log can also include comments or activities. For example, a secondary school reading log might ask for eight entries per year (or two per quarter); each entry in the log needs to include a brief reflection on the particular book, and one or two of the eight entries needs to include a task, such as an essay, animation, or other project, to demonstrate a depth of knowledge about the selection. You might also require that the reading log include a range of genres from both fiction and nonfiction. Going beyond the required number of entries can earn a student a next-level badge; if eight selections are needed for a bronze badge, perhaps 10 or 12 are required for a silver badge, the next level badge.

Tasks in Listening and Speaking

Some schools decide that the best thing to concentrate on in a portfolio are skills that are *not* well covered by existing exams. These might include listening and speaking skills.

Although you may offer assignments that you preface with "focus on your writing," you may not offer many that start with "focus on your listening." Still, listening skills are crucial. Can the student interact with other students as part of a group project or class discussion? Does the student listen for information in school, gaining the needed information? Is the student able to watch an instructional video and figure out how to apply those skills? Being able to retrieve new ideas from a video is a key assumption behind many flipped classroom or online class initiatives. It may well be worth your time to develop tasks where students can demonstrate their mastery in this area.

Speaking tasks are more common; the formal presentation in front of a class is still a component of many curricula. However, the tasks to earn a speaking badge can go beyond the traditional. Contemporary tasks can include the use of various media, ranging from effective use of slideshows to creating a podcast or video presentation. The audience can consist of a small group in a classroom, or, if the presentation is web-enabled, the speaker might address a sister school across the globe. The formats can range from a small-group discussion (where we see the student demonstrating *both* listening and speaking skills); to a persuasive argument as part of a debate; to a science-fair type stand-up description of work (with questions and answers); to a TED-style talk. (Figure 3.3 shows an example of this speaking task; the student in the video is the same student reading in Figure 3.2, 11 years later.) Students are using their speaking skills all the time in schools; to earn a badge, they should be able to capture any number of these events and describe how they fulfill the requirements the school has laid out.

This brings up a point about the tasks that appear in the portfolio. Let's say that in social studies, students are asked to engage in a debate around a current event. The task is a social studies task, but the student may see this

FIGURE 3.3 | **High School Speaking Task**

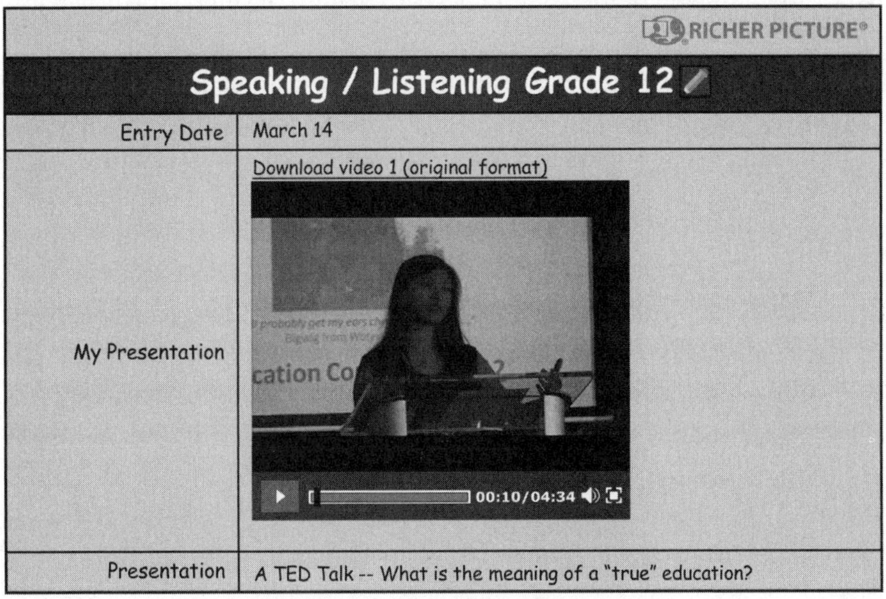
RICHER PICTURE®
Speaking / Listening Grade 12
Entry Date
March 14
Download video 1 (original format)
My Presentation
00:10/04:34
Presentation
A TED Talk -- What is the meaning of a "true" education?

Source: Copyright © 2018 Ideas Consulting, Inc. Used with permission.

as their best demonstration of their speaking skills. It's worthwhile for both students and teachers to look for these *incidental tasks*; they provide more opportunities for students to fulfill the badge requirements without creating any additional work.

Tasks in Mathematics

In many ways, mathematics is our most traditional area of the curriculum. Much of the content traces back to the ancient Greeks—and it can feel like much of our pedagogy traces back that far as well. There is a grand elegance to mathematics; as a field, it begins with some fundamental concepts, from which everything else can be derived. Whole numbers lead to counting; counting leads to arithmetic; division leads to fractions; fractions lead to decimals and percentages; rational numbers lead to irrational numbers. What we understand about points leads to understanding lines and on to triangles, quadrilaterals, pentagons, hexagons, n-agons, circles, three-dimensional objects, and so on.

But this elegance can be lost along the way as the rules get more abstract. We lose many students when working with fractions; how is it that dividing by a fraction means flipping the fraction and multiplying? The concrete rules of basic arithmetic have given way to something that seems arbitrary. Students can learn how to do the algorithm to get the right answer, but they start losing an understanding of the rules. For other students, the arbitrariness comes later. As one student put it to me, "I liked math until the numbers turned into letters."

Moving toward digital badges and portfolios is an opportunity to think about what your school truly values in mathematics education. Many states have adopted a set of math practices that cut across all areas of the math curriculum. For example, Ohio's Standards for Mathematical Practices (Ohio Department of Education, 2017) are as follows:

- Make sense of problems and persevere in solving them.
- Reason abstractly and quantitatively.
- Construct viable arguments and critique the reasoning of others.
- Model with mathematics.
- Use appropriate tools strategically.
- Attend to precision.
- Look for and make use of structure.
- Look for and express regularity in repeated reasoning.

Note that these practices can apply from elementary arithmetic to advanced placement calculus.

So what tasks should go into a math portfolio? In one school, teachers noted from their standardized test score data that their students were generally fine in computational ability but were having trouble with word problems. Thus, the school decided to focus their portfolio energies on problem-solving skills. Specifically, students were asked to demonstrate those skills by making a video and walking through how they solved a problem.

In this elementary school, students regularly completed a "problem of the week." These were typically word problems, such as the following:

> It is said that dogs age seven years for every "people year." Mason's dog, Shep, was born on Mason's 8th birthday. When Mason was 9 years old, Shep was 7 dog-years old. In dog-years, how old will Shep be on Mason's 12th birthday? (Exemplars, 2017)

To earn the badge, the students selected one of their completed problems. Each student then sat with the teacher and walked through the problem. The student was asked to (1) retell the problem in their own words; (2) list an "I need to ..." statement, which described the strategy for solving the problem; and (3) walk through their actual work. These conversations with the teacher were recorded.

The recording shows the problem-solving process at work. We can see whether the student fully understands the problem. The "I need to" statement indicates whether the student has a good starting point, and the process of showing the work indicates where the student is in regard to the actual mathematical capacity. Essentially, what the video will reveal is the student's ability to figure out what information is relevant or irrelevant and what mathematical tool will be most useful to address the problem. This kind of task can be done at any grade level and can show growth in problem solving.

Of course, there are many other tasks involving math that can go into the portfolio. From geometry scavenger hunts, where students take pictures of geometric concepts in their neighborhood, to measurement tasks, such as determining the total area of all the windows in the cafeteria, to statistics projects, such as looking at the percentage of families with school-age children over time, math portfolios can contain far more than worksheets. The key to determining which tasks should fulfill the badge is determining which skills we most want students to demonstrate.

Tasks in Science

The leading science journal *Nature* posited that "global scientific output doubles every nine years" (Van Noorden, 2014). Sometimes, it feels like the science curriculum is expanding at the same rate.

Certainly, it's exciting to be able to access the latest developments as soon as they are published and use the same data that scientists across the world use for their research. But it's also overwhelming. Just as the student at the beginning of this chapter noted, it's all too easy to reduce science to a mere set of vocabulary tests.

The process of predicting, making observations, collecting data, analyzing the results, and drawing conclusions is still at the heart of the scientific method, and this process can occur across all the grade levels. A science badge, then, can be associated with tasks that let students demonstrate their ability to walk through this process.

The Next Generation Science Standards have defined a set of *cross-cutting concepts* similar to the math practices defined by the National Council of Teachers of Mathematics (2000). The following concepts occur throughout the various scientific disciplines (NGSS Lead States, 2013):

- Patterns
- Cause and effect
- Scale, proportion, and quantity
- Systems and system models
- Energy and matter
- Structure and function
- Stability and change

Moreover, the Next Generation document provides sample performance expectations for each of these concepts. These are organized by grade level; students in grades K–2 can show an understanding of patterns through "observations of the sun, moon, and stars to describe patterns that can be predicted" (1-ESS1-1), whereas high school students "Construct and revise an explanation for the outcome of a simple chemical reaction based on the outermost electron states of atoms, trends in the periodic table, and knowledge of the patterns of chemical properties" (HS-PS1-2). These performance expectations provide samples of the kinds of tasks a student can complete in order to earn the badge.

Of course, tasks aren't limited to just those found in standards guidebooks or textbooks. Students can focus on their observational skills or their ability to analyze data by, say, looking at weather data over the course of a week. Students can participate in independent projects such as science fairs or simply do a smaller-scale project in class.

Tasks in History/Social Studies

As with science (and most other disciplines), any attempt to "cover" the social studies curriculum can be crushing. This is another example of the comment from Grant Wiggins (1989) about "the futility of trying to teach everything of importance" (p. 44).

This may be a good time to bring up the work of Jay McTighe, who has thought deeply about tasks and assessments for many years. Specifically, I'd like to focus on what he calls *transfer goals* and *cornerstone tasks*.

When we think about badges and portfolios, we are trying to get to the heart of each subject area. The transfer goals are our aspirations; students who leave a class should be able to take the skills and knowledge they have gained and apply them in another setting. In most subject areas, a small number of overarching transfer goals can drive the curriculum.

In history, for example, the transfer goals could look like this:

> Students will be able to independently use their learning to
>
> - Apply lessons of the past to current and future events and issues, as well as to other historical eras.
> - Critically appraise political, social, and historical claims/decisions in light of available evidence and reasoning. (McTighe, 2017)

These can also be put in the form of essential questions:

- How do events in the past inform our understanding of the present—and our ability to shape the future?

- How do we evaluate a political, social, or historical claim? What evidence and reasoning will convince us?

There's a pattern here. Like the math practices and the Next Generation Science crosscutting concepts, the transfer goals can be used throughout all the grade levels. To earn a badge, then, is to demonstrate some proficiency with these transfer goals. The tasks can be the cornerstone tasks, which McTighe characterizes as follows:

The Cornerstones are curriculum-embedded tasks that are intended to engage students in applying their knowledge and skills in an authentic context. Like a cornerstone anchors a building, these tasks are meant to anchor the curriculum around the most important performances that we want learners to be able to do (on their own) with acquired content knowledge and skill....

More specifically, cornerstone tasks

- Are curriculum embedded (as opposed to externally imposed).
- Recur across the grades, becoming increasingly sophisticated over time.
- Establish authentic contexts for performance.
- Call for understanding and transfer through genuine performance.
- May be used as rich learning activities or assessments.
- Integrate 21st century skills (e.g., critical thinking, technology use, teamwork) with subject-area content.
- Evaluate performance with established rubrics.
- Engage students in meaningful learning while encouraging the best teaching.
- Provide content for student portfolios so that students graduate with a résumé of demonstrated accomplishments rather than simply a transcript of courses taken. (McTighe, 2017, p. 21)

If you are a social studies teacher, look at the tasks you ask students to complete. Which of these meet the criteria of a cornerstone task? Those are your most likely candidates for the portfolio.

One example of a cornerstone task that recurs is an investigation—for example, why are the biggest cities in the world located where they are? At the elementary level, students can look at the geography of the American East Coast or the Australian southeast and consider why the particular geography of New York or Sydney made those cities more likely locations for settlers. At the secondary level, students can start with a chart like the one shown in Figure 3.4, which shows the census population for two neighboring California counties: the city and county of San Francisco and the county of San Mateo (just south of San Francisco, including what we now call Silicon Valley). What might explain the changes in growth over the last 100 years? What might make either location attractive to settlers now?

Another common task is the DBQ, or *document-based question*, popularized in advanced placement history courses. Essentially, these ask students to analyze various primary documents. Some variations of this task are simply reading comprehension exercises; a teacher might give a student the text of Martin Luther King Jr.'s "Letter from a Birmingham Jail" and ask, "What are King's arguments about why segregation is unjust?" Certainly, comprehending the text is a prerequisite for analyzing it, but simply restating the argument doesn't make this a cornerstone task.

FIGURE 3.4 | **Sample Graph for Social Studies Task**

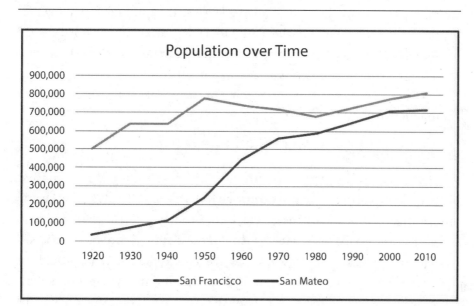

For it to become a cornerstone task, we need to make it more authentic and tie it more directly to our transfer goals. So that they more fully understand King, we could ask students to compare the letter to past documents. These might range from Roger Williams's "A Plea for Religious Liberty" or Benjamin Franklin's "Petition from the Pennsylvania Society for the Abolition of Slavery," to documents from the 1960s on the topic or documents written by today's leaders. Students could then discuss how the notion of civil rights has permeated American history.

Tasks in World Languages/English as a Second Language

The study of second languages addresses the same issues of reading, writing, speaking, and listening discussed earlier. For a portfolio, it may be most useful to focus on student growth and proficiency in the language over time. Making recordings of student progress in speaking and listening several times during the year will enable students to see the improvement in their vocabulary, pronunciation, and precision.

The American Council on the Teaching of Foreign Languages (ACTFL) has a set of standards that guide the development of tasks. The World-Readiness Standards for Learning Languages (ACTFL, 2015) has organized standards around the 5 C's: communication, culture, connections, comparisons, and communities. The standards suggest that an understanding of a second language is rooted in the ability to communicate but that it's critical for students to be able to "interact with cultural competence." The tasks that stem from these standards should allow students to show their communication skills as well as their understanding of the people with whom they are communicating.

Tasks in the Arts

Portfolios have been present in the arts forever; in some ways, the concept of the educational portfolio was borrowed from the arts. The tasks in the arts are naturally performance based. Thus, performing and visual arts teachers can easily gather a list of candidate tasks for the digital portfolios and badges.

The basic question comes back to the requirements. What would we like to see in *every* student's portfolio? Can students simply select three best pieces from any arts course they happen to take? Do we want to see a breadth of various performances, or do we want to see growth along a particular dimension (or both)?

We've seen in earlier examples that some schools set up choices for students; a student can earn an arts badge by completing a badge in music, visual arts, theater, dance, or some other form of expression. One strategy that can work well is to have the arts educators define what every student should know and be able to do and establish requirements that ensure that every graduate has the ability to create and critique. What's important, though, in creating these requirements is understanding that students can complete them in any number of settings—in arts or music classes in school, in lessons outside school, in community arts projects (such as singing in a church choir), or by effectively using the arts across the disciplines.

Arnold Aprill (2010) has described a "false dichotomy" in the arts, pitting "direct instruction vs. arts integration." Schools do not have to decide between one or the other. Arts educators can work with other teachers in the school to help ensure that all students in the school meet the arts requirements. For example, in one elementary school, a project that focused on the essential question "How do we observe?" joined the arts and science curricula. Students participated in projects, such as drawing trees outside the school at different times of the year or creating detailed illustrations of leaves to show how the shapes and vein structures vary.

Defining the tasks for any badge can open up possibilities for collaboration across the curriculum. Badges in writing don't have to be limited to English; badges in problem solving aren't just the sole domain of math. If we're truly interested in working with the whole child, then there should be opportunities for students to achieve many badges during any class.

Tasks in Technology

Technology is a broad term; for the moment, let's focus on computer technology. It's worth dividing the demonstration of technology skills into two areas: (1) the use of technology to support all the other inquiries and tasks and (2) the tasks that are about understanding the technology itself.

In the first case, consider the use of computer technology for presentations. Throughout the grade levels, students are creating slideshows to support presentations in history or science or business classes. Typically, the assessment of the presentation focuses on the subject-area content. When done well, though, the technology can make the content clearer or the speech more engaging. The use of technology in this instance might be enough to help the student earn the technology badge as well as fulfill the requirements in history or science or business.

Other tasks have technology as the center. A technology badge requirement could also include mastery of a common application, like a spreadsheet, or proficiency in a programming language. The ISTE Standards for Students (International Society for Technology in Education, 2016) has been used by many districts as the heart of a technology curriculum. The standards are designed to be flexible and are rarely tied to specific hardware or software, meaning that the tasks you use for the technology badge can be managed with the equipment you have in place.

One popular technology task actually began outside the classroom. The popularity of robotics over the last decade has been an interesting phenomenon. Initially inspired by Seymour Papert's seminal book *Mindstorms* (1980), schools started acquiring special Lego kits with programmable bricks. The first projects were based on those that came with the kits; students would build Ferris wheels or other demonstrations of physical movement. Things dramatically ramped up with the development of the FIRST Robotics Competition, in which students were given a challenge (such as locating a pair of glasses within a designated playing field) and school teams came together to see if their robots could complete that challenge. In many schools, the project started as a club, where a teacher advisor would gather some interested students together after school and work on the robots for the competition. Eventually, many schools began offering courses in robotics in the curriculum.

What's interesting is that the curriculum has changed because of student interests. The growth in robotics courses didn't come from a top-down development of a robotics curriculum. The movement from after-school club to full-fledged course speaks to another way of developing tasks for the digital badges and portfolios. Ask the obvious question: What do students want to do?

Tasks in Career and Technical Skills

Many career and technical fields have specific certifications, offered either by the government or by the industry. For example, the National Institute for Automotive Service Excellence has a process for certification that any high school can use. The guidelines for such certificates can guide the tasks that students need to complete; the portfolio and badges can show the overall progress that students are making. For example, a student may complete the tasks related to engine repair before moving on to automatic transmissions.

Even in fields without specific certifications, tasks can stem from the overall program expectations. What are the range of skills we would expect from a student studying culinary skills or organic farming? These skills can define the tasks needed for fulfillment of the badge.

In Chapter 2, we mentioned career pathways. Here, a pathway might ask a student to combine badges from different disciplines. A music production pathway could include both a performance badge from the music department and a badge in music technology, which might require a student to produce a piece of music to be used as the audio track of a presentation or video.

Tasks in Physical Education and Health

There are plenty of tasks from physical education and health classes that are badge worthy, but I also suggest *observation* as a task. Many of the goals of these classes have to do with habits and choices. Take the remonstration to "live a healthy lifestyle." Although individual tasks can demonstrate efforts toward that goal, such as developing a healthy eating plan, much can be seen in moment-to-moment choices. Trying out for a team, making more effort in gym, or showing up a little earlier for school may also be useful signs of a healthy lifestyle.

Many physical education teachers and coaches keep an observation log; they note when a student has tried something new or met a personal best. Adding these observations to the digital portfolio can create a new category of tasks. If a teacher observes a certain behavior multiple times—say, three observations of good teamwork—then the student could get credit for completing a task.

Tasks in Special Education

For special education students, the portfolio offers an interesting opportunity to focus on student growth. To show that growth, we might include a task, such as a writing sample, each quarter or each month, not just one or two times per year. Special education teachers regularly think about the kinds of tasks (with appropriate accommodations) that will help their students show their success. Being able to show the milestones of a goal attainment scale can provide a more complete picture of what the student is working on and what the student has already achieved.

In many ways, the development of mastery learning is actually an extension of how special education has always been arranged. A team of teachers, family members, and the student figure out the learning goals; the teachers and students work together toward those goals. The education is personalized and occurs at its own pace, with accommodations as necessary. The movement toward personalized, competency-based learning takes this same concept and applies it to all students.

Earning Badges Based on Data

Some badges may be earned through accomplishments besides classwork. For example, students could earn a badge based on good attendance, using data you are already collecting. Some data, such as absences or tardies, might be used to fulfill a work habits badge. Other data, such as course grades, could indicate growth over time. A diary of hours spent each week on schoolwork or personal reading might be a demonstration of effort toward achieving an academic badge.

There's also the matter of standardized test data. If you want to use test scores as a component of a badge requirement, it's only fair to ensure that the test you're using is appropriate for that purpose. For example, most standardized tests focused on language arts skills will provide some evidence of reading comprehension or on-demand writing skills. Few deal with extended writing prompts, and none with speaking or listening skills. Thus, any use of that test score to fulfill a badge needs to correspond to the appropriate subject areas. In short, you need to consider whether this particular test score truly shows whether the student has fulfilled the requirement for this badge.

Earning Badges Through Projects

Project-based learning has become quite popular as of late. Certainly, the idea of taking a concept and exploring it in more depth is an attractive way of showing student skills. But just as with classroom tasks, we need to ensure that the projects are portfolio-worthy.

The Buck Institute for Education has developed a useful schematic called the Gold Standard for project-based learning. John Larmer, John Mergendoller, and Suzie Boss (2015a) propose the following criteria for examining projects:

- The project centers on *key knowledge and understanding* and *key success skills*.

- The project answers a *challenging problem or question* and requires *sustained inquiry*. It's important to note the difference between a task that takes a long time and a project. If a middle school student is asked to count the number of milk cartons that the school uses each day, that might take a long time, but it isn't a project in itself. If the student, however, is asked to use this data to answer a larger question, such as to determine how much space could be saved in landfills by recycling those cartons, then the student is answering a challenging problem.

- The project has *authenticity*. This can include real-world authenticity—for example, the challenge of getting more people to use the subway is an authentic problem, whereas the traditional "two trains are leaving a station in opposite directions…" is probably not. It is also important to consider personal authenticity, meaning that the project is of concern to the students themselves.

- The project is designed with *student voice and choice*. The amount of choice might vary, but even the most basic projects should allow students to have some level of ownership.
- The project offers opportunity for *reflection*.
- The project allows for *critique and revision*.
- The project will produce a *public product*; that is, the student will create something, be it a tangible product or a presentation, that can be viewed and discussed.

When done well, there can be a clear line from the project to the goals to the badge. That is, the student knows that after successfully completing the project, he or she will have fulfilled at least one of the requirements toward the badge.

Of course, projects can take place within the regular class time. For example, at one elementary school, students worked on an interdisciplinary project related to observation. In science class, students learned about different ecosystems, such as the desert or rainforest; then, with an artist-in-residence, the students created drawings of those environments based on their readings and observations.

Although projects typically require more class time than typical classroom tasks, they enable students to address a concept or area of inquiry in more depth—which also allows teachers to observe student progress over a longer period of time. That longer time also allows the student to potentially work toward multiple badges simultaneously. For example, the rainforest project would help fulfill both the arts and science badges.

Student-Initiated Tasks and Projects

Tasks and projects are often generated by the teacher. Schools can ensure more personalization by making space for student-initiated projects. The capstone project, in place in many schools, offers such an opportunity.

At Narragansett High School, students learn about the senior project right at the start of their freshman year. The work begins in earnest in the fall of the senior year as students think about the project they want to pursue. They're asked to write a proposal that describes how this project will be a learning stretch. It also needs to meet the following criteria:

- Your senior project should be one that engages and excites you. This is an opportunity for you to explore something entirely new or push your skills even further in an area where you already excel.

- A learning stretch expands your knowledge and skills in your topic area. It asks you to challenge yourself. Your new knowledge should extend well beyond your current level of expertise, but still be within your reach. (Narragansett High School, 2014)

Once they have a confirmed topic, students create a *sign of commitment*. This is a small poster that students put up in the school's media center, illustrating every project. Not only do these posters enable each senior to describe his or her project, but they also show the rest of the students the range of possibilities for senior projects. The signs show a great variety of interests, from creating a musical performance to developing an app to learning how to become a sports announcer. Other projects stem from topics studied in class, from environmental changes to creative writing to agriculture.

Over the course of the year, the students meet with a mentor, complete a time/cost analysis, conduct fieldwork, and write a research paper. All these steps are stored in the digital portfolio.

There are several advantages to keeping track of a project in a digital portfolio. First, everything is in one place. Some students need help getting organized, and having a location for each component is useful. Second, teachers can keep track of student progress. The senior project coordinator at Narragansett generates reports to ensure that students have completed each component and can tell if there are teachers or students who may be a bit behind.

Perhaps the biggest advantage comes at the end of the project. At Narragansett, the final step of the senior project is the presentation. Students are asked to present their work to a panel, which includes school faculty and administrators as well as community members (which may include parents, school board members, mentors, or others). Before the presentation, the panelists are given a login where they can see the student projects that are on their presentation schedule, along with each project's components. Students see that their work is being presented in a professional manner; they can set their best foot forward and let the work speak for itself. To conclude the process, the panelists assess the project using a rubric; a passing assessment can then fulfill the senior project badge.

Student-initiated projects do not need to be a year-long capstone; they can be measured in days or weeks. In any case, students need to discuss the project with someone if they want to use it to earn credit toward a badge. Schools with strong advisory programs can make this happen quite easily, and a discussion with an advisor can help shape a meaningful project.

Quests

Another version of projects is the quest. As described by Jacobs and Alcock (2017), the quest provides a structure for thinking about projects, as shown in Figure 3.5.

FIGURE 3.5 | **Contemporary Quest**

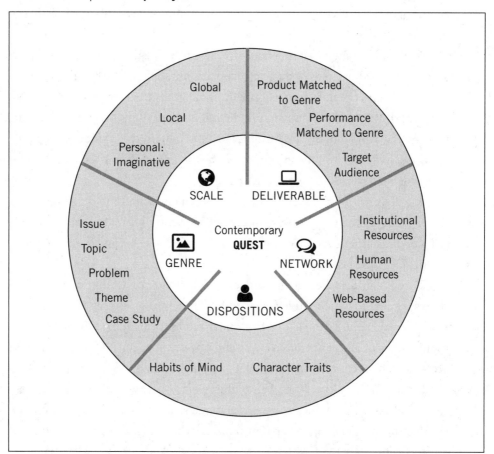

Source: From *Bold Moves for Schools: How We Create Remarkable Learning Environments* by H. H. Jacobs and M. Alcock, 2017, p. 80. Alexandria, VA: ASCD. Copyright 2017 by Heidi Hayes Jacobs and Marie Hubley Alcock. Reprinted with permission.

Although a teacher can design a quest, the structure is very student-friendly. It helps for the student to first think about the *genre* of the quest—specifically, one of five categories:

- Topical (a quest for information)
- Issue (a quest to explore an issue)
- Problem (a quest to solve a problem)
- Theme (a quest to connect ideas)
- Case study (a quest to pursue skills or knowledge in depth)

For example, a student who expresses an interest in environmental science might start with a topical quest to identify the key issues in the field. The student could then decide if this would have a global, local, or personal scale: What environmental issues have arisen most frequently in local or state legislatures in the last year? Or what environmental issue is the most visible to me and my family?

Students can then link this quest to various badges. Some may be subject-area badges; others may focus on dispositions, such as the habits of mind. Students then complete a mission statement that describes what they plan to do, what they plan to deliver, and how long they think this will take. This focuses the work on the *deliverables*—the products the students will ultimately deliver—as well as on the *network*—the list of resources that the student will need to create those deliverables.

In a digital portfolio system, the quests can be accumulated into a library. Other students can peruse these quests and potentially create their own variation of one of them. A collection of well-designed quests can be the backbone of a project-based curriculum.

Quests can also be set up with prerequisites. For example, Figure 3.6 shows a quest in which students learn how much solar energy is required to power a rock band. To engage in this quest, students must first finish two prerequisite tasks: a task on solar power and one on electricity. Once those tasks are successfully completed, the rock band quest is unlocked.

If this sounds like a video game, then you've got the right idea. A course can be set up as a sequence of quests arranged in a set of paths and branches; completing one quest opens up new paths for the student to discover and new quests to complete.

FIGURE 3.6 | **Unlocking Quests**

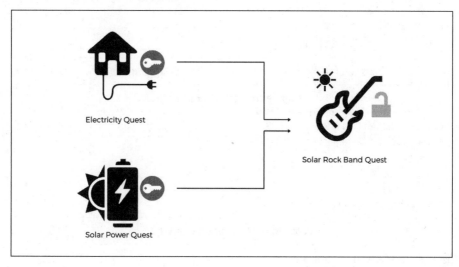

Validating Tasks

Your teachers have now selected the tasks they want to use, ranging from basic on-demand tasks to full-blown projects and quests. What happens now?

To help ensure that faculty members are on the same page, consider running a validation exercise as part of your professional development. To begin, teachers start with the form they completed (Figure 3.1) that identifies the tasks they plan to use.

One variation of the tuning protocol (Allen & Blythe, 2004) is to have the faculty divide into groups of three or four, with the teachers from different departments in each of the groups. Teachers do a round-robin, where each one is, in turn, a presenter and the others are reviewers.

First, the presenter goes through the list of identified tasks. This provides some context; the teacher can describe how these three or four tasks fit in the overall flow of the course. Then the presenter looks at one of the tasks in depth, displaying the associated rubric and any other relevant materials. If sample student responses are available, the teacher can also show these.

To respond to the presenter, the reviewers can use the form shown in Figure 3.7, which focuses attention on four key areas.

Let's consider each area in turn.

First, what is the task assessing? It's important to identify the competencies being addressed; even if it seems obvious to the person designing the

FIGURE 3.7 | **Assessing Task Design**

Task discussed: _____

Grade: _____ Subject: _____

Questions to Ask	What Suggestions Do We Have?
What is the task assessing?	

• What competencies are addressed?
• What educational goals are addressed?
  ○ Knowledge
  ○ Basic skills
  ○ Understanding
  ○ Long-term transfer	

Is the task clear and engaging?	
• Is the task engaging for students? • How much student choice is built into the task? • Are the directions clear, thorough, and concise? • Do the instructions and supporting materials provide clear expectations for quality work?	
Is the task rigorous and authentic?	
• Do students have the skills required to complete this task? How will they learn/practice those skills? • Are students required to use complex reasoning skills (explain, justify, challenge, synthesize, etc.) in a context that is true to the discipline? • Is the task authentic? That is, does the performance assessment require thinking at the heart of the discipline?	
Is the feedback useful?	
• What feedback/rubrics will you use? • Assessing the work: Are the scoring criteria clear? • Is there distinct differentiation among performance levels?	

task, it may not be obvious to the reviewers (and, thus, to the students). It also helps to identify the *type* of educational goals that are being addressed. Using the types highlighted in the Understanding by Design framework (Wiggins & McTighe, 2011), teachers can identify whether the assessment is aiming at *knowledge, basic skills, understanding,* or *long-term transfer goals*. Note that all of these are important; we need basic skills goals as well as long-term transfer goals. What is most crucial is seeing whether the assessment truly meets the stated goal. If the aim is for long-term transfer of mathematical problem solving but the task explicitly lays out all the steps, are the students going to be able to demonstrate the appropriate skill level? Put simply, in the words of Jay McTighe (2018), "Does this task assess the things that matter?"

Second, is the task clear and engaging? It helps to know if students are going to be able to figure out what they're being asked to do with the task. Now *clear* doesn't mean that every step has to be laid out; in fact, in terms of including student voice, some of the details cannot be written down because the students themselves will be generating them. Rather, *clear* simply ensures that students receive the information they need. Similarly, *engaging* simply means that the task will make use of students' skills and knowledge—and perhaps provide an opportunity for exploration, creativity, and imagination.

Third, is the task rigorous and authentic? This gets to the qualities of tasks. If the task is tied to specific badges, can the presenter make the compelling argument that this task is indeed worthy of this badge? The Depth of Knowledge scale (Webb, 2002) can also be useful to determine if this is a worthy task.

Finally, is the feedback useful? The rubric needs to be clear about expectations (we will look at good rubrics in more detail in the next chapter). Certainly, it's worth verifying that the rubric is actually measuring the things that the presenter says are the most important elements of the task. For example, if the student is asked to create a slideshow on a topic, does the rubric have the appropriate focus on both content and presentation?

The reason for engaging in a cross-curricular validation exercise is to encourage teachers to focus on the task, rather than the content. It's fine that math teachers are looking at art tasks, and vice versa; the idea is to take the presenter's task and determine whether it's worthy, based on the presenter's explanation of what's important. That is, the presenting teacher needs to make a compelling defense. This is not to say that the reviewers' job is to sit in judgment; rather, this is meant to be a cooperative exercise. Offering suggestions for improvement is a crucial part of the process.

In addition, going interdisciplinary can help teachers—particularly at the secondary level—get a better sense of what is being asked of students in other areas. Students often lament that teachers don't understand what else is going on with them; here, teachers can get a glimpse of the kinds of tasks that are a part of the other courses. This, in turn, starts to set a gauge of the degree of difficulty. Many teachers coming from these review protocols start to consider whether they might need to make their own tasks more rigorous.

Tasks: Best Work for Both Students and Teachers

When done well, introducing portfolio-worthy tasks can make the classroom more exciting. As students work through these tasks, the focus of the classroom shifts from teachers being the center of attention to students fulfilling their task requirements. As we will see in Chapter 6, other things have to change to support the implementation of these tasks. Nevertheless, setting up these portfolio-worthy tasks gives both students and teachers an opportunity to show their best work.

Effective Feedback
with Schoolwide Rubrics

How do we decide what is "good" or, at least, "good enough"?

Feedback is the most important component of any digital portfolio or badge initiative. The interaction between teacher and student determines whether your initiative will be successful. More than the planning, the policy incentives, and the specific technology platform, the most crucial decision you'll make in creating your digital portfolios and badges is determining how students will get feedback on their work.

Researchers have noted the importance of feedback for a long time. The work on *authentic assessment* in the 1980s and 1990s (see, e.g., Darling-Hammond et al., 1995; McDonald, Smith, Turner, Finney, & Barton, 1993; Wiggins, 1998) described many schools that began rethinking assessments. Whether it was an urban high school looking to strengthen student writing or a suburban elementary school experimenting with new forms of conferencing, the success went beyond developing new tasks. Having someone paying attention to students and their work was a crucial common thread.

Many schools go through the motions of setting up digital portfolios, training everyone on the new software and making sure that teachers are recording their tasks and that students are uploading their artifacts. The schools where teachers and students buy into the initiative understand there has to be a payoff for their efforts. If students make the effort to put together portfolios of their best work, they need to receive more than just a check in the gradebook.

The essential question for thinking about feedback is this: How do we decide what is "good"—or, at least, "good enough"? If a digital badge is going to have any credibility, there must be a shared understanding of what it means to earn the badge and a shared understanding of the quality of work expected of students. When defining the requirements, it's important to establish the boundaries between what's acceptable and what isn't there yet—in other words, to define the level of "good enough."

Just as important, the essential question deliberately uses the word *we* ("How do *we* decide…?"). Faculty need to come to a common agreement about what work is acceptable, and this understanding needs to be shared with students and parents.

In this chapter, we'll look at three techniques your school community can use to put a shared vision into action: schoolwide rubrics, calibration, and reflection (both student and teacher). These tools will not only help you reach that common understanding of what it means to earn a badge (and, in essence, demonstrate mastery), but also help you provide better feedback for your students.

Schoolwide Rubrics

Rubrics have been around for a long time, but they have become much more widespread as a form of assessment in the last 20 years or so. The motivation is clear enough: Having an established, written set of criteria for an assessment makes it easier for teachers and students to specify what kind of work "meets the standard."

As is usually the case, though, the devil is in the details. The development of rubrics hasn't always meant that things are clearer. Some rubrics are written so vaguely that the assignment of a "1," "2," "3," or "4" seems arbitrary; some rubrics are so specific that grading becomes nothing more than an exercise in counting red marks.

As long as rubrics were limited to the quirks of an individual classroom, nothing much needed to change. To implement badges for a school and a district, however, we need assessment techniques that work across multiple teachers, multiple grade levels, and, potentially, multiple schools. We need common, or schoolwide, rubrics. (Or, what you're really after might be a districtwide or department-wide rubric. Feel free to substitute those words for *schoolwide* if that's more appropriate for your site.)

Sample Common Rubric

For schoolwide rubrics, consider tasks that occur often in different classes and with different teachers. For example, let's look at the rubric shown in Figure 4.1, which corresponds to the Next Generation Science Standard for "scientific investigations."

This rubric is designed to be used for any scientific investigation. Whenever a student submits a task as evidence that is linked to this standard, all teachers agree to use this rubric to determine if the student work should count toward the badge. Thus, for any investigation done in biology, physics, or earth science—whether the class is considered honors or not, whether the students are in 9th grade or 12th grade—teachers use the same rubric.

Figure 4.1 shows five rows areas to assess: "hypothesis," "data," "discussion/analysis questions," "conclusions," and "organization." These, of course, correspond to the typical sections of a lab report. The complete rubric also has additional rows and indicators for components such as Graphs and Calculations, which are not shown here; depending on the specific lab, some rows may be omitted. The overarching idea, however, is that the rubric is written to accommodate a variety of tasks yet also provide a consistent tool for assessment.

The last row of the rubric, Organization, includes one indicator in each column that is specific to the lab report format and one indicator that is used throughout the school for all kinds of written reports. Students will see the same indicator about applying "the rules and mechanics of writing" on rubrics used in English or social studies or anywhere else the student is generating a report. Among other things, this sends a message that writing mechanics count throughout the school.

What's also noteworthy about this rubric is what's missing. The specific content of the investigation isn't mentioned. The Discussion/Analysis Questions row indicates that each student needs to correctly answer the questions, using examples from the data. The language of the rubric enables the teacher to ask for different types of analysis, depending on the lab. For example, one classroom task asks students to identify and illustrate (with video examples) each of Newton's Three Laws of Motion. The task could require students to analyze how each illustration connects to that law. Another task from chemistry, asking students to identify an unknown compound, could require students to enumerate the tests they performed to determine the components of the compound and to analyze the results of each test.

FIGURE 4.1 | **Rubric for Scientific Investigations**

Student creates a scientific lab report by identifying a problem, predicting an outcome, collecting data, and analyzing and evaluating results.

	Exemplary: 4	Proficient: 3	Developing: 2	Beginning: 1
Hypothesis	Generates a sophisticated, plausible, tentative solution that uses an "if… then… because" statement	Generates a plausible, tentative solution that uses an "if… then… because" statement	Generates a flawed tentative solution that uses an "if… then…" statement, but omits "because…"	Generates a flawed tentative solution that makes little sense *or* Does not use an "if… then… because" statement
Data	Organizes and obtains information in an appropriate format that is easy to read and understand and is error free Information collected is relevant to the procedure including quantitative and qualitative data	Organizes and obtains information in an appropriate format that is easy to read with minimal errors Information is relevant to the procedure	Organizes and obtains information in a format that may be difficult to read or has significant errors Some information may be irrelevant to the procedure	Organizes and obtains information in a format this is unreadable Much of the information is irrelevant to the procedure
Discussion/ Analysis Questions	All answers to discussion/ analysis questions are answered correctly and insightfully and include multiple examples from data Offers well-constructed suggestions for solving similar problems in the future	Answers to discussion/ analysis questions; may have one or two minor errors that don't detract from overall understanding and include examples from data Offers well-constructed suggestions for solving similar problems in the future	Some answers to discussion/ analysis questions are answered incorrectly and use few, if any, examples from data in answers Offers one or a limited suggestion for solving similar problems in the future	Several answers to discussion/ analysis questions are answered incorrectly and do not have any examples from the data Offers no suggestions for solving similar problems in the future

	Exemplary: 4	Proficient: 3	Developing: 2	Beginning: 1
Conclusions	Compares what student knows now with what was known prior to conducting the investigation by describing specific parts of the procedure or data that contributed to learning Sophisticated discussion of how what was learned in the lab applies to the course's essential question. Student provides specific examples	Compares what student knows now with what was known prior to conducting the investigation Discusses how what was learned in the lab applies to the course's essential question	Student fails to compare what was learned with prior knowledge Discusses either what was learned in the experiment *or* how the experiment applies to the essential question	Fails to establish what has been learned by conducting the investigation Seriously flawed attempt to connect what was learned in the lab *or* the connection to the essential question
Organization	Follows prescribed lab report format with little or no guidance Skillfully applies the rules and mechanics of writing making no errors	Follows the prescribed lab report format Consistently applies the rules and mechanics of writing making occasional errors	Attempts to follow the prescribed lab report format Applies rules and mechanics of writing making frequent errors	Does not follow the prescribed format Inconsistently applies the rules and mechanics of writing, making many errors

Source: Ponaganset High School, Foster-Glocester Regional School District, Rhode Island. Used with permission.

This speaks to one of the challenges in creating schoolwide rubrics: how to be specific enough to provide useful feedback but general enough that students recognize the important elements they need to demonstrate. The wording of each indicator allows different teachers to include different task-specific elements in their assignments but still be able to use the common rubric.

This suggests one way of building a schoolwide rubric. Ask teachers to meet, bringing any rubrics they have. In this case, the members of the science department can all bring their own lab report or scientific investigations rubric to the conversation. Then the group can separate the indicators into two categories: the *common* indicators and the *task-specific* indicators. The common indicators are ones that are included in more than one rubric or are applicable to more than one task. Those common indicators are the candidates to include in the schoolwide version of the rubric.

Including Task-Specific Indicators

But what are we to do about the task-specific indicators? Researchers at the Stanford Center for Assessment, Learning, and Equity (SCALE, 2017) have suggested creating a *look fors* section in the rubric. Consider the focus on the practice "construct viable arguments" shown in the math rubric in Figure 4.2.

Two things are worth noting. First, the row includes the "sources of evidence." That is, when teachers are assessing this work, students know where the teachers will be looking. The score for "construct viable arguments" will come from the student's response to a given question—here, Question 1. Second, the bottom row contains the task-specific indicators, references to the "area of the base of the garden box"; the Advanced column includes the indicator of "Provides more than one strategy."

These additions to the rubric allow the teacher to add information that will help the student connect the rubric to the task at hand. This makes scoring easier for the teacher while maintaining the integrity of the common rubric.

When done well, a conversation around the schoolwide rubrics will echo the conversations about badges and tasks from the previous chapters. In each case, the focus is on the end goal: What do we want our students to know and be able to do? A schoolwide rubric articulates the qualities you are looking for in that work and, as such, can require a deep conversation about what is most valuable about the task and what you most want to see in your students' performances.

Anchors

Many other common rubrics are available through state and provincial departments of education, through textbook publishers, and on various peer-sharing websites. It's easy to do a search for rubrics in any number of content areas and find hundreds of examples. What's trickier is to determine which rubric will actually be useful across multiple teachers and (potentially) multiple grade levels.

FIGURE 4.2 | Sample Practice from Math Rubric, with Look Fors

Practice	Emerging	E/D	Developing	D/P	Proficient	P/A	Advanced
Construct Viable Arguments *Source of Evidence:* *Question 1*	I am still working to provide evidence (that someone else will understand) to support my conjectures, arguments, and claims.		I provide partial or inconsistent evidence to support my conjectures, arguments, and claims.		I support my arguments and claims with evidence. I evaluate and improve incomplete or flawed arguments.		I provide more than one way to verify that my argument is correct.
Look Fors	• Explanation is flawed and would not result in correct approach to calculating the area of the base of the garden box.		• Partially explains how to either ** decompose the figure *or* ** use negative space to calculate the area of the base of the garden box.		• Thoroughly explains how to either ** decompose the figure *or* ** use negative space to calculate the area of the garden box.		• Provides more than one strategy.

The "6+1 Traits of Writing" developed at Education Northwest (2014) identify key components of writing: ideas, organization, voice, word choice, sentence fluency, conventions, plus presentation. These elements of writing cut across all genres—narrative, argumentative/persuasive, reflective, and creative. Using this rubric consistently means that students will become more familiar with the criteria and thus start to internalize these elements in all forms of their writing.

One version of the rubric is designed for grades 3–12. In the Frequently Asked Questions section of Education Northwest's website, the top question, not surprisingly, is "How can one rubric address writing across such a wide span of years?" Education Northwest's advice is to use *anchor papers* to accompany the rubric. As you and your colleagues start to use common rubrics, it can often help to collect these anchors or benchmark performances to illustrate what a score of "4," "3," "2," or "1" can look like. In her book *How to Create and Use Rubrics for Formative Assessment and Grading*, Susan M. Brookhart (2013) shows how one school illustrated the six traits by including a sample piece of work from each level. Benchmark performances can be useful for teachers as they assess the work and for students as they look for models. (Of course, you will want to ensure that any student work that gets shared has identifying information removed; we'll revisit this more in the section on calibration.)

Potential Pitfalls

Rubrics are meant to provide students and teachers with clear criteria about what's important in the task. All too often, though, the language doesn't help to differentiate the levels. For example, many rubrics will have indicators that begin with *all*, *most*, *some*, and *none*:

	4	3	2	1
Paragraphing	Paragraphs are well organized.	Paragraphs are mostly organized.	Paragraphs are somewhat organized.	Paragraphs are not organized.

But when does a text move from being "somewhat" organized to "mostly" organized? Students have no clear indicators that can inform them of the difference.

Sometimes there's a willingness to allow for vague indicators because this enables individual teachers to preserve their own judgments. In other words, each teacher can define what *somewhat* and *mostly* means. Ultimately, though, this defeats the purpose of having a "common" rubric. A common rubric should represent a vision of what is important to demonstrate and should be clearly understood by all teachers and students.

As you work through the rubric indicators, push to make your language more specific. If this causes some conflict within the group working on the rubric, it's best to get these points of view articulated at this early stage. (The calibration protocol, discussed in the following section, can help schools analyze their rubrics and help teachers come to a common understanding of what they should be looking for.)

Also, consider the column headers at the top of many 4-point rubrics:

	Exceeds Expectations	Meets Expectations	Below Expectations	Little or No Evidence
Criteria				

This clearly sets a differentiator between the second and third columns: "meets expectations" is acceptable; "below expectations" is not (and clearly the last column indicates that no attempt has been made at all).

Let's look for a moment, however, at the "below expectations" column, which refers to work that makes a real attempt but doesn't meet the desired level of quality. Often, it's exactly those students who could use the most guidance. If the student tried but did not succeed, what could he or she do differently next time? The rubric should indicate this.

One way to think about the rubric is to change the column headers as follows:

	Exceeds Expectations	Meets Expectations	Needs More Work	Needs More Instruction
Criteria				

The column headers shift the focus in the two right-hand columns to what the student needs to do to improve. "Needs more work" indicates that the student essentially understands the concepts and skills involved but that this particular entry falls short. The student could use more practice or put more energy into an aspect of the entry to move the score into the acceptable range. The "needs more instruction" column indicates that the student is misunderstanding a concept or, perhaps, entirely missing a concept. More practice, by itself, will not lead this student to move up the scale; the student needs some additional guidance and study to achieve at the acceptable level. By using these column headings, the rubric focuses more on what the student *needs* rather than on what the student *lacks*.

Another alternative is to define the rubrics based on badge levels. For example, the column headers can be as follows:

	Gold Level	Silver Level	Bronze Level	Beginning Level
Criteria				

Many schools, in creating their schoolwide rubrics, define the "acceptable" level as the level required for graduation. That is, a score of "3" on the schoolwide rubric is the level expected of a student exiting the school (at grades 5, 8, or 12). By itself, that's fine; it establishes the expectations for every student who walks across the stage. But when schools start to apply that rubric for *entering* students, many students are (unsurprisingly) not at a "3" level. Although teachers certainly don't expect students to be at graduation level at the beginning of a given year, realistically students may be discouraged by initially seeing that they aren't "passing."

Some teachers make up for this by giving a numeric score separate from the rubric score, but this can send a mixed message. A student could think, "I got a 70 on this task so I passed, but the rubric says I'm 'not achieving at standard.' Which do I believe?" This isn't just some mild confusion; this double standard can affect the quality of schooling. As Rick Stiggins (2017) points out, three decades of research on assessment *for* learning has confirmed what many teachers know instinctively: "A student's emotional response to assessment results will determine what that student decides to do about those results: keep working, or give up" (p. 85).

Thus, although graduation rubrics are absolutely helpful in defining where we want students to be at the end, schoolwide rubrics can also be used to define milestones along the way. Gold, silver, and bronze speak to varied levels of accomplishment—that is, although the gold level may seem intimidatingly unachievable for most students in the first year, the silver and bronze levels celebrate various degrees of success, as opposed to such ratings as "meets expectations" or "below expectations."

Finally, as you write the rubrics, remember to keep the language student-friendly, but not at the expense of precision. If the task at hand is to develop a hypothesis, there's nothing wrong with using the word *hypothesis* in the rubric, even if it's the first time students are encountering that word.

Some schools run into trouble by taking language straight out of a state standards document that is written for adults and placing it unchanged into the student's rubric. Most elementary teachers will, out of habit, revise the language using age-appropriate vocabulary. But teachers in higher grades may not think to do so.

Consider a middle school standard for Speaking and Listening from the Common Core State Standards (National Governors Association Center for Best Practices, Council of Chief State School Officers, 2010):

> Delineate a speaker's argument and specific claims, evaluating the soundness of the reasoning and relevance and sufficiency of the evidence and identifying when irrelevant evidence is introduced. (CCSS.ELA-LITERACY.SL.8.3)

To make this more student-friendly, a teacher might put it this way: To meet this standard, a student should be able to

- Retell a speaker's overall argument.
- Describe the evidence the speaker uses to support the argument.
- Determine if this evidence is sound.
- Determine if this evidence is relevant.

In this case, the original language is broken down into multiple short points and recast with a simpler vocabulary. You might make other changes (e.g., using the word *convincing* instead of *sound*). It's certainly worth discussing if the simpler language conveys the same meaning as the original. Nevertheless, a rubric is not useful if students can't understand it.

As you develop your rubrics, SCALE's checklist for Quality Rubric Design can be helpful (see Figure 4.3). Of course, before building your rubric, you'll need to determine both its primary purpose—is it summative or formative?—and its primary audience—is it for students, teachers, or both?

As a final point, consider having student work in front of you as you write the rubrics. Look at different levels of performance. What is the difference

FIGURE 4.3 | **SCALE Checklist for Quality Rubric Design**

Purpose: Learning-Centered Design

☐ Rubric **sets clear expectations**: Describes proficient performance.

☐ Rubric is **analytic**: Performance is broken down into distinct dimensions.

☐ Rubric is **educative**: Provides feedback to teachers and students to support learning and improvement.

☐ Rubric is **common**: Can be used within and across courses, grade levels or grade spans, tasks, and teachers to measure progress toward long-term performance outcomes.

Content

☐ Rubric is tightly aligned to key performance outcomes.

☐ Rubric measures worthwhile knowledge and skills: standards-aligned content, complex disciplinary understandings and practices, and 21st century skills.

☐ Rubric is not task-specific; generalizes to a variety of tasks within the discipline.

Structure and Organization

☐ Rubric is short for usability and focus.

☐ Dimensions are distinct and focused, with few indicators within each performance level.

☐ Dimensions are sequenced in a logical order.

☐ Indicators should not be grouped together within a single performance level if student performance on those indicators often varies.

☐ Indicators are not repeated across dimensions.

☐ Indicators for each performance level are parallel in sequence and grammatical style across the dimensions.

Performance Levels

☐ Performance levels reflect a developmental progression through qualitative (vs. quantitative) differences in student performance.

☐ Rubric has a sufficient number of performance levels to capture progress within a grade level or grade span, and especially in the range where the majority of students fall.

☐ Rubric uses standards-based criteria to define proficiency.

Language

☐ Performance-level labels and indicators are neutral in tone and avoid value-laden, stigmatizing language.

☐ Rubric describes observable behaviors and skills in the work sample; describes what students *can* do and *not* what they can't do.

☐ Language is simple, clear, and provides clear distinctions between levels; is student-friendly.

☐ Rubric communicates how a student can get to the next performance level.

Source: Checklist for Quality Rubric Design, Stanford Center for Assessment, Learning, and Equity (SCALE), 2017. Used with permission.

between the acceptable paper and the unacceptable one? This can help you find the best language to use in the rubric's indicators.

Calibration: Working Together on Assessment

Using schoolwide rubrics is often something new for teachers. Many teachers are used to creating their own assignments and are protective of their assessment practices. After all, they are the ones assigning the grades, and they need to be able to defend those scores when asked by students or parents. On the other hand, this approach can make assessment feel arbitrary; we know that Ms. B may give an *A* to a project that Ms. K would give a *C* to. Even more so, teachers and schools have been accused of grade inflation, giving better scores to work that would have been considered below standard in earlier times (Hurwitz & Lee, 2018).

Schoolwide rubrics address this issue of arbitrariness. Through the use of common language for the assessments, teachers should be looking for the same things in the student work. If a student submits the same work to different teachers—all of whom use the same rubric—the student should get the same score almost all of the time. The school can start to demonstrate a level of consistency in how certain tasks are assessed.

One technique for helping to achieve a level of consistency is *calibration* (also known as *moderation*). Essentially, a calibration exercise involves a group of teachers; everyone in the group scores a few pieces of student work using a common rubric. The group then comes to a consensus about the scores to determine what qualities constitute a "1," "2," "3," or "4" on each row of the rubric. The idea is that the teachers will agree on what they'll look for so when they assess the rest of the student work individually, they'll be able to give scores consistent with those their colleagues give. This way, the school can feel secure that badges are being awarded fairly, no matter who is doing the assessment.

Let's walk through the protocol in a little more detail. You need to do three things in preparation for the calibration. First, decide on the task you want to use. If your school is big enough, this could be a task that all of the teachers in the group have assigned in their classes—for example, a common writing assignment for all 8th grade history classes. If you don't have such a task, look for one that *could* be given by all the teachers in the group; for example, a science department could look at a biology investigation, even if not every person in the group is teaching biology this year.

Second, assemble your groups. An ideal group would have four or five members—large enough for a variety of opinions, but small enough so that everyone is heard. It's crucial that every participant walk away from the session with a deeper understanding of the assessment.

Third, select the actual student work that will be used in the calibration. You can ask one teacher to bring several examples or have several teachers each provide one example. For the calibration to be useful, the samples should show a range of performance, but they should not, at least for this exercise, be at the far ends of the spectrum. If you choose a stellar piece of work, most likely everyone in the group would agree it's fantastic. The best strategy is to select a couple of samples where the question "Is this work good enough?" might actually generate debate. (If you're using a 4-point rubric where a score of "3" passes, try to select at least two samples that could be a "2" or a "3" and another sample that could be a "3" or a "4.")

When possible, make the student samples anonymous by hiding the student names. This isn't always feasible (such as when the samples are videos of student performances), but if you can do it, it's worth the effort. Now, with the work selected, the calibration process can start.

Step 1. Individually Score the Work

Each person in the group receives a copy of the assignment, the student work samples, and a copy of the rubric for each student sample. The moderator of the exercise goes over the task and rubric, describing the context. For example, "This task took place just before the midterm when students began to synthesize the content from the course. They had two days to complete the assignment. They worked in groups, but each turned in an individual submission."

Each participant then scores the samples individually. The teacher should have a separate rubric/score sheet for each of the samples. At this point, the teachers shouldn't be discussing the work with the other participants.

Step 2. Discuss the Evidence

Once this is done, the teachers begin the discussion. For each criterion (i.e., row) of the rubric, the teachers should look at the samples. The moderator leads with the question "What evidence led you to the score you gave on this row?" One important piece of advice here: *Do not reveal the actual scores.* This discussion is about bringing up what each teacher noticed in the work. For example, "I really looked to see if the student's hypothesis statement used language I thought the student truly understood, rather than just words copied from the textbook; that's what determined whether I gave the sample a low or a high score."

There's a reason for going over the evidence *before* going through the scores. To take an example from another field, consider a phenomenon in criminal trials. Researchers investigating how juries come to decisions noted that when a jury takes a vote early in the deliberations—on average, within the first 10 minutes—the jurors are *less* likely to come to a final verdict (Hannaford-Agor, Hans, Mott, & Munsterman, 2004). It is possible that revealing a decision too early in the process puts participants in a position of having to defend that initial decision.

A recorder for the group of teachers should note on chart paper or a projected screen the various pieces of evidence that the participants used to come to a decision. By doing so, the group is creating a set of "things to look for" in all of the student work and whenever they use this rubric after this calibration is completed.

It's worth going through all of the rows first, looking at the evidence that led to the various decisions. It's not unusual for participants to note that a decision on one aspect of the student work led to a specific score on more than one row. In other words, some aspects struck certain teachers as more important than others. That's what we want to tease out; the ways that a particular piece of work is striking (either positively or negatively), and what that means for the score. This process can also help the group understand what aspects are the most important and how much weight any one aspect should carry. A teacher who has, say, spent more time with a class on finding the right voice might be more sensitive to that aspect of a student's writing than another and thus may be assessing the work through that filter to the point where it affects how the teacher is scoring all the rows of the rubric.

Step 3. Agree on a Consensus Score

Once all the evidence is on the table for all the samples, the group needs to come up with a common score. That is, group members need to assume that the student who wrote Sample A will be given one final marked-up rubric. What should the scores on that rubric be?

This is the point at which the participants reveal their scores. They do not have to stick with the scores they originally marked in Step 1; the conversation in Step 2 can add new perspectives and thus change the scores. In an online version of the calibration protocol, using Richer Picture software, after all of the participants have added their scores, each person can see a collective rubric (see Figure 4.4). This shows which indicators were selected and how many participants highlighted each cell. As you can see, a score of "3"—"meets standard"—garnered the most votes for this particular sample.

FIGURE 4.4 | **Calibration: Collective Scores**

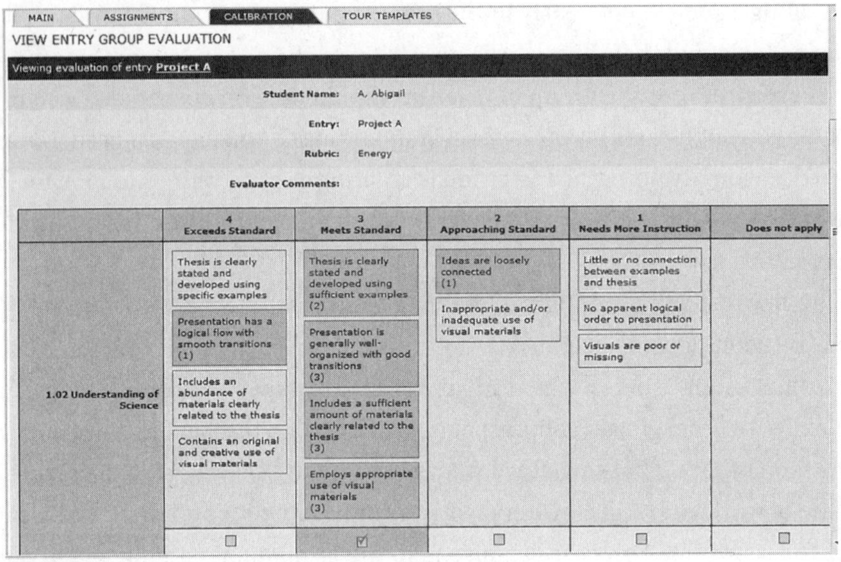

Source: Copyright © 2018 Ideas Consulting, Inc. Used with permission.

There are various ways to come to consensus. The key here is that each person in the group needs to understand *the group*'s rationale for giving a student performance a given rating. This discussion should lead to a consensus of what it means to "meet" the standard and thus provide a blueprint for assessing other work with the same rubric. The calibration process is summarized in Figure 4.5.

The Many Uses of Calibration Protocols

As schools become more comfortable with the calibration process, it is possible to create some deeper variations. For example, if teachers are using a schoolwide rubric for scientific investigations, a calibration group could use samples from different courses—say, a biology, a chemistry, and an earth science investigation. Can the teachers come to a consensus about what's an acceptable level of work across a diverse set of tasks?

FIGURE 4.5 | Summary of Calibration Protocol

Time	Steps
10–15 minutes	**Step 1. Individually score the work.** Each person • Reads the assignment. • Reads the rubric. • Scores each of the sample responses using the rubric. • Does *not* reveal scores to the other participants.
Up to 5 minutes per criterion (row)	**Step 2. Discuss the evidence.** The group • Goes through each criterion (row) of the rubric. • On chart paper, answers the question "What evidence led you to give your scores on this criterion?"

10 minutes per sample	**Step 3. Agree on a consensus score.** After completing all of the rows
	• Select one of the sample responses.
	• For each row of the rubric
	  ** Reveal your scores.
	  ** As a group, come up with a consensus score—that is, the group needs to decide on *one* score for each row.
	  ** As a group, decide on the comment you will collectively give to the student for this row.
	• Repeat for each sample.

The calibration protocol can also be used for pilot-testing new rubrics. A teacher might volunteer to use a newly developed schoolwide rubric with a specific task that he or she has assigned. After students have turned in the task, the rest of the faculty can use a calibration exercise and determine whether the rubric is clear enough. If there is a great deal of variation in the scores—or if, during the Step 2 discussion, teachers say that they weren't clear about what evidence to use to come up with a score—then it's possible that the rubric could use some tweaking.

Another use of the calibration protocol is to help new teachers become part of the school community. The idea isn't to see whether the new teachers match the scores given by previous groups, but rather to see whether the new group (even if there's only one new member) will come to a new consensus. Providing new teachers with a voice in the conversation is helpful.

Finally, calibration protocols can help students understand the rubric. In this case, you may wish to look at samples of student work from other schools or districts. Rather than just telling students, "This is what a '3' looks like," the students can look at samples and, through the Step 2 conversation, begin to understand what it takes to achieve the criterion and, ultimately, receive the badge.

Self-Assessment and Reflection

John Dewey, the great philosopher of education, wrote extensively on the importance of reflective thought. His work is often paraphrased into the simple aphorism "We do not learn from experience... we learn from reflecting on experience." Dewey's actual words cut deeper. As Dewey wrote in his seminal *How We Think* (1933),

> Of course intellectual learning includes the amassing and retention of information. But information is an undigested burden unless it is understood.... —a result that is attained only when acquisition is accompanied by constant reflection upon the meaning of what is studied. (p. 177)

If you've been in education for any length of time, you've heard the importance of going beyond rote memorization. From Bloom's taxonomy to higher-order thinking skills to Costa and Kallick's habits of mind and the other habits we discussed in Chapter 2, most teachers have been exposed to the concept that students can learn deeply and that schools need to encourage this. The reality, however, is that schools are incredibly accepting of students attaining just a superficial understanding of the curriculum.

In sports, the arts, and other performance areas, we encourage students to practice certain fundamental skills until they become second nature. The act of dribbling a basketball or placing one's hands on the piano at middle C isn't an inborn skill, but after sufficient practice, students will start to do these things automatically.

In the traditional academic subjects, we similarly want a set of skills to become second nature: the rules of grammar, the multiplication tables, the ability to find your home country on a map. And, indeed, it is truly helpful for attaining upper-level skills to have these skills be automatic. This means getting drilled on these skills and practicing and practicing them.

Yet this same approach to learning is applied to more advanced topics. Algebra classes spend weeks factoring and graphing quadratic equations. Students practice the skill repeatedly, with the successful students picking up speed and following the steps with more agility.

Here's the fatal flaw, though. Just because a student has memorized a fact or practiced a skill doesn't mean that the student has understood it—at least, in the sense that Dewey used the word *understanding*.

The issue isn't just the use of drill and practice. Even the most engaging project-based curriculum can fall short here; students might use math in a project, but if the math simply requires plugging figures into a formula, then the student's takeaway of math skills could be very fragile.

Reflection, in the context of digital portfolios, is meant to reinforce learning, similar to how an addition of concrete reinforces a building. After completing a task, students should comment on what they learned and on how this task is providing evidence that they are closer to earning a badge.

At least, that's the idea in theory. In reality, when students are first asked to reflect on their work, their responses are often not very deep. We see responses such as "This is a good piece of work because I got a good grade on it." Or we'll see samples of circular logic, such as "This is a good example of problem solving because I solved the problem." In one class in which I observed, some students were whispering to one another, "What does she [the teacher] want us to say?" as if the reflection was meant to be another graded component of the assignment.

The reflection prompt helps a great deal. Rather than a vague "Please reflect on your work," ask something more specific like "What strategies did you use to complete this task? How do you think you could use those strategies in the future?" This can help students focus on the skills they used and think about how those skills might be transferrable.

"What did you find easy about this task? What did you find difficult?" asks students to consider their strengths and weaknesses. "What advice would you have for another student completing this task?" can get the student to consider the perspective of someone who wasn't present when this task was completed and thus requires the student to explain what is necessary in more detail. There are many other good reflection prompts for all grade levels, such as "40 Reflection Questions" published by Edutopia (2011).

How often is it necessary to reflect? Initially, schools asked students to reflect on each entry that went into the portfolio, assuming the portfolio would contain three to five entries for each student from each full-year class. However, many teachers find it difficult to provide useful feedback on so many reflections.

One way around this is to ask students to focus reflection on the collection of work. At the end of each individual task, the student can add a brief comment or note at the end of each task, focusing perhaps on what they learned that was new or what was easy or difficult about the task. This note does not have to be submitted as part of the entry. Then, when a student completes a badge, the teacher can ask the student to reflect on the entire body of evidence that is being used to demonstrate the badge requirements. The notes on the individual entries can feed into this overall, end-of-badge or end-of-year reflection.

One strategy to help students reflect on their learning is to ask them to evaluate their own work using the same rubric as the teacher. This certainly encourages the students to read through the indicators of the rubric. To do a proper self-evaluation, the student should have evidence of why the scores on each row are justified. Whether you ask students to articulate this reasoning in writing is another matter, but having the students mark up the rubric will show that they are (hopefully) looking for the same things you are to determine if the work meets the criteria.

The self-evaluation doesn't have to be accepted by the teacher as a final grade, but it can form a center of conversation. If a student and teacher come up with wildly different scores on the rubric, it's worth exploring why. Do the student and teacher have different ideas of what the rubric criteria represent? Is the student focused on some aspect of the performance to judge the scores ("I worked really hard on this assignment, so I deserve a good grade")? If many students are coming up with scores that are different from the teacher's, is there some common misunderstanding of the rubric that needs clarification?

In the end, self-evaluation is part of the process of assessment that can support your digital badge and portfolio work. The keys to good assessment are feedback and communication. Ultimately, you'll have a successful assessment system if the answer to the essential question "What is good enough?" is shared across all of your students and teachers. If everyone understands the goal, it's so much easier to reach it.

Tours: Student Presentations of Portfolios

How do students present their best work?

Imagine that you're a painter. You've been at it for a few years, and you've created a fair number of paintings, which you keep in a collection. Every now and again, you are asked to show a sample of your work. A potential client might want to meet with you about painting a portrait; when you go to that conversation, you select some of your best portraits, reflect on what makes your work unique, and present those portraits to your potential client. At another time, you might have an opportunity to show your work at a coffee house or local library; this time, you select a different combination of work, including portraits, landscapes, and abstract pieces, that show the range of your skills.

The process of generating digital portfolios asks students to "collect, select, reflect, and present" their best work (Niguidula, 2006). Creating the digital portfolio takes a while, but where portfolios gain their power is in the conversations they generate.

At the elementary level, parent-student-teacher conferences are an opportunity for students to show how they have grown as a learner. At the secondary level, students being able to discuss their *body* of work makes for a conversation that doesn't often happen in many high schools. Being able to look across multiple entries and projects and reflect on progress is a skill we need to be encouraging in schools, and it's one that can prove valuable beyond school life. In Charles Duhigg's popular book on productivity, *Smarter Faster*

Better (2016), a vice president of a major technology company says, "We look for people [to hire] who describe their experiences as some kind of a narrative. It's a tip-off that someone has an instinct for connecting the dots and understanding how the world works at a deeper level."

In this chapter, we'll explore *tours*—student presentations of their portfolios. We'll look at the kinds of tours your students can construct as they curate their own narratives, and we'll examine different ways that you can arrange the tour presentations.

The Badge Tour

The badge tour structure consists of two parts, the first of which is **evidence**. The entries for evidence can be classroom tasks, logs (such as reading logs or community service hours), projects, or data points (such as attendance). For example, Figure 5.1 shows that the student has met the requirements for the badge in geometry through conducting a scavenger hunt and by creating an animation. The reader should be able to go to the requirements component of each tour and see the specific examples that the student has selected to fulfill the badge.

FIGURE 5.1 | **Badge Tour: List of Evidence**

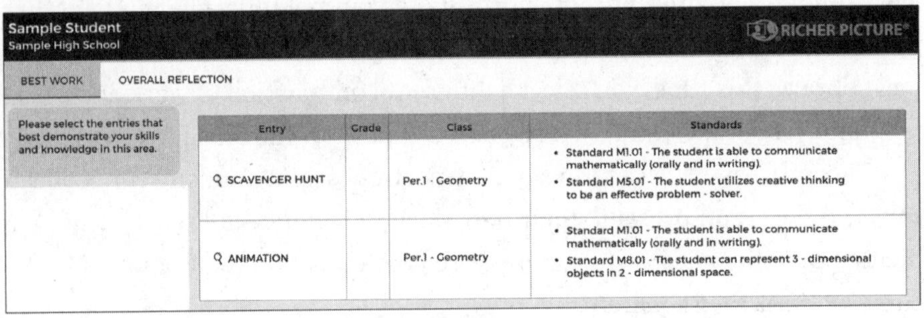
Sample Student
Sample High School
RICHER PICTURE®
BEST WORK OVERALL REFLECTION
Please select the entries that best demonstrate your skills and knowledge in this area.

Entry	Grade	Class	Standards
SCAVENGER HUNT		Per.1 - Geometry	• Standard M1.01 - The student is able to communicate mathematically (orally and in writing). • Standard M5.01 - The student utilizes creative thinking to be an effective problem - solver.
ANIMATION		Per.1 - Geometry	• Standard M1.01 - The student is able to communicate mathematically (orally and in writing). • Standard M8.01 - The student can represent 3 - dimensional objects in 2 - dimensional space.

Source: Copyright © 2018 Ideas Consulting, Inc. Used with permission.

Student choice is important here. In the great majority of cases, students can select the pieces they want to use as demonstrations of their best work. They can decide what constitutes best work—and then change their minds later. Consider the math example; perhaps halfway through the year, the student has a great sample for geometry that she wants to include as evidence that she has fulfilled the goal. And so, she puts it in the tour. Later, she has another example that she prefers; the new entry then replaces the old one.

In other words, tours can be built over time. It might help students—particularly when the badges have a number of requirements—to have milestones, such as "select one entry for your tour by the end of each semester."

The second part of the badge tour is the **overall reflection**. Here, the student writes a brief description about the collection of entries and describes why these entries are valid evidence toward demonstrating the badge requirements. The reflection here is not about an individual entry, but about the *body* of work that the student has submitted.

For example, Mt. Hope High School in Rhode Island has students respond to the following prompts when describing their skills as a problem solver:

- What are the skills or strategies you use to be successful in problem solving and critical thinking?
- How do the pieces you've included in this section highlight your strengths in this area?
- How will these skills help you in the future?

This reflection prompt has a deliberate order. First, the student is asked to think about problem solving in general terms. We want the student to understand what he's actually demonstrating; in this case, what does *problem solving* mean to the student in his own experience?

Second, students are asked to tie the entries in the work to their understanding of what problem solving is. Framing the prompt to have the student explain the concept first helps the student think about the entries as **specific examples of a general skill**. The idea is that when the student writes the answer to this prompt, she will need to think about how she applied this skill in the various entries.

Along the same lines, this second prompt also asks students to "highlight your strengths." This prompt encourages students to think about their new skills and knowledge as strengths and to consider the earning of this badge as an accomplishment.

The third prompt, "How will these skills help you in the future?" gets directly at Jay McTighe's focus on transfer skills that we discussed in Chapter 3. The prompt turns around the old student lament "How come we have to do this, anyway?" by asking the student to come up with their *own* reasons about why these skills could be useful down the road.

Students may not always have the best answers to these prompts. It may not be obvious to them how the problem-solving skills they have learned in, say, Algebra II will apply beyond a school setting. Nevertheless, student responses to this prompt can help us as educators understand how they're defining "the future" and help us see if they're able to make a connection between today's work and their plans for tomorrow.

Reflections usually require practice. When students at any age are first asked to reflect on their work, they often don't know where to start. Teachers themselves are often unsure what makes a good reflection, and you may even find some who aren't convinced that reflection is actually useful at all.

Some years ago, I was talking to a middle school student who was asked to reflect on her writing skills. The school had adopted a version of the "6 Traits" rubric for writing, which they used consistently over the year. The rubric had a scale from 0 to 5, and the teachers averaged the scores on the six rows together to get an overall grade. A score of "4" was considered passing.

Here's what the student wrote as a reflection:

My grade was a 3.8. Overall, that's pretty good. The grading was fair. It was a little tougher than last time, but it can't be the same every time. I'm going to use the grades the grader gave me to help my writing.

I felt pretty good about the grade I received. Sure, I'm a little disappointed in myself but 3.8 isn't that bad. It's only 2 points below a passing grade, which is a 4.0. I feel that I could have tried a little harder. I didn't give 100% effort. Well, I'll just need to focus more in the future.

For the next writing assessment, I'm going to try to achieve a 4.2. I want to get that grade or higher because it is in between my previous grade, which was a 4.6, and the grade I just received, which is a 3.8.

I'm going to work on my conventions because that is the lowest score I got, which is 3. Another point I want to work on is my spelling and grammar because that is what I messed up on in the assessment. Hopefully, I will reach my desired goal.

Now this reflection is clearly a response to a set of questions. We can see that the student was asked to comment on whether she thought the grading was fair, how she felt about the grade, what she hopes to do next time, and what specific area she will focus on. These are a perfectly fine set of questions.

However, this student is focused on the numbers. In each section of the response, she mentions her grade; she's thinking about her next goal simply as a numeric target: the average of the past two scores. What this reflection *doesn't* have is a lot of insight. It's not a bad reflection; it's just one that could be modified to help show the path forward.

As part of our work with this school, we asked the student to do another reflection on the work. This time, though, rather than having the student write it out, she and I just talked.

Q: Is writing something you find easy? Is it something you find hard?
A: When I have an assignment and I really want to write about it, then I'll express all my feelings and I'll get to the subject and I'll write a good paper. If it's something I'm not as interested in, I'll still write the paper, but I won't have as much voice as in a paper I'd want to write.

Q: What kinds of topics make you interested? What do you like to write about?
A: Topics where I could express how I feel about them like [pause]… we just wrote one about the things students do to misbehave in class. I mean, I can relate to that because I'm in the class while they're misbehaving, and I know what they're doing.

Q: What kind of writing do you think you do the best on, when it comes to these different traits?
A: I think organization because I always get those paragraphs strong and transitions because I can get from one paragraph to the next one and putting it all together.

Q: What area do you think you need to work on the most?
A: Voice, because I think I need to put more of my point of view in my writing.

This reflection brings out something different. Here, the student is articulating an insight; when asked if she finds the general idea of writing to be easy or hard, she describes how it's sometimes easy and sometimes hard, and she mentions (without prompting) that she finds the writing easier when she's interested in the topic. Her discussion of the traits from the rubric doesn't bring up numbers at all; she feels clear about where her strengths lie—in organization and transitions—and what she needs to do to improve.

This whole conversation took 90 seconds. Many teachers have these mini-coaching sessions all the time to help students with needed skills. A writing teacher will walk around as students are working; a brief conversation with one student about using synonyms to help with word choice may be followed by a chat with another student about how the evidence she uses in one paragraph is stronger than in another. These one-on-one conversations can be profound, and they can help the student get on the right track. The personal guidance may also help to fortify why the reflections are needed in the first place.

Similarly, students may need some coaching in deciding what entries to put into the tour. I have found this is especially true the first time the school introduces tours or portfolio presentations. Students don't necessarily have a vision of what the tour is supposed to look like; the mental model isn't in place. Looking at samples or taking a little more time to guide students as they create their first tours can pay off in the long run.

The End-of-Year/Term Tour

At certain set points in time, such as the end of the year or the end of the term, students can prepare a tour of the best work they've done in this time period. A tour based on time usually focuses on a breadth of entries. Students might select, say, one entry from each class they've taken this year. They then discuss the work with an audience.

This form is often used in elementary schools. A student-led conference might happen at the end of the first and third quarters of the year. The tour will contain entries from that part of the year; a student might have a sample of reading, writing, science, social studies, music, and physical education.

The temptation for the student is just to describe each entry. It's helpful to provide some guidance on an appropriate reflection. The student should tell a story: This is about my growth as a learner. What do each of these entries say about me as a student? What do these entries have in common?

Many high schools do not have the equivalent of a student-led conference. Let's describe how some schools have handled this.

The Best Work Tour

Students select their best work from the year and reflect on it. There are often three sections:

1. **Cover.** Include a picture or video welcoming the reader to your portfolio.

2. **Best work.** Sample prompt: Please select your four best pieces of work from this year. Each entry must have received a score of "3" or better on the schoolwide rubric. Your pieces should all come from different classes.

3. **Reflection.** Sample prompt: Please describe why you think each of these pieces represents your best work.

One simple way to get started is to ask students to select their best work. One student's choices are shown in Figure 5.2.

FIGURE 5.2 | **Tour: Selecting Best Work**

Selected		Entry	Class	Complete	Artifacts	Scores	
☑	🔍	Scavenger Hunt	Per. 1 - Geometry	✓	4	Math 1.1	3
						Math 1.3	4
☐	🔍	Coordinate Task	Per. 1 - Geometry	✓	1	Math 1.1	3
☑	🔍	Contour Lines	Per. 2 - Art / Drawing	✓	1	Arts 2.2	3
☐	🔍	Abstract	Per. 2 - Art / Drawing	✓	1	Arts 2.1	3
☐	🔍	Create a Creature	Per. 3 - Biology	✓	2	Sci 1.1	3
☑	🔍	pH Lab	Per. 3 - Biology	✓	1	Sci 1.2	4
☐	🔍	Lewis & Clark Project	Per. 4 - US History	✓	1	Soc 2.2	4
☑	🔍	Interactive Maps	Per. 4 - US History	✓	3	Soc 2.1	4
						Soc 2.2	4
☑	🔍	Persuasive Argument Podcast	Per. 5 - English 10	✓	1	Speak 1.2	3
☐	🔍	Reflective Essay	Per. 5 - English 10	✓	1	Writ 1.4	3
☑	🔍	International Exchange	Per. 6 - Spanish II	✓	3	Speak 1.3	3
						List 1.1	4

Source: Copyright © 2018 Ideas Consulting, Inc. Used with permission.

In this example, the first prompt is simply, "Your Year End Review should include your best work toward achieving mastery in each of the six core areas: English, math, science, social studies, the arts and technology." In Figure 5.2, we see that the student has selected six tasks from different classes. In this case, the only restrictions for the student selection are that the work come from this current school year and that the entries received a score of "meets expectation" (a score of 3 out of 4) or better on any of the schoolwide rubrics.

In the right-hand column of Figure 5.2, the student and teacher can see the scores to verify that each entry meets these criteria.

To be effective, the best-work portfolio needs to be accompanied by some kind of reflection. Once the student has selected the entries, he or she can include a written statement or brief video clip as the reflection. The reader should read this statement or watch this clip before looking at the individual entries.

The Action Plan Tour

Let's consider another example, this one from Mt. Hope High School. The end-of-year review has several sections:

1. Cover
2. Personal statement
3. Requirements summary (a report showing all the entries added to the portfolio this year)
4. Action plan
5. Best work
6. Work related to my interests and goals

At Mt. Hope, the end-of-year presentation is a conversation between the student and two teachers. The teachers are teamed up by the school's portfolio coordinator, who sets up the teams so students are grouped with at least one teacher they know and so that the two teachers bring different perspectives. They're often from different departments, and newer teachers are typically paired with veterans.

Students begin their tours with a **personal statement**. Because the students may not know both reviewers, the personal statement provides an introduction to who they are and highlights both their interests and their personal and career goals. Students also use the statement to describe their progress as a learner. The statement may only be a few paragraphs long, but it can help put the work in context. As the name states, the *personal* statement is a way of making this tour more personalized.

Following the personal statement is the **requirements summary** (also known as the *completeness* page), as shown in Figure 5.3.

The completeness page is simply a report automatically generated by the software. Mt. Hope's version of the page has two parts. The top part shows the student's list of classes. The reviewer can see how many entries have been added and how many were marked as acceptable—that is, deemed by the classroom teacher to have met the standard. The page shows that all the artifacts have been uploaded and that the requirements for a given entry have all been completed.

FIGURE 5.3 | **Requirements Summary (Completeness Page)**

Class	Entry	Complete	Artifacts	Scores	
Per. 1 - Geometry	Scavenger Hunt	✔	4	Math 1.1	3
				Math 1.3	4
	Coordinate Task	✔	1	Math 1.1	3
Per. 2 - Art / Drawing	Contour Lines	✔	1	Arts 2.2	3
	Abstract	✔	1	Arts 2.1	3
Per. 3 - Biology	Create a Creature	✔	2	Sci 1.1	3
	pH Lab	✔	1	Sci 1.2	4
Per. 4 - US History	Lewis & Clark Project	✔	1	Soc 2.2	4
	Interactive Maps	✔	3	Soc 2.1	4
				Soc 2.2	4
Per. 5 - English 10	Persuasive Argument Podcast	✔	1	Speak 1.2	3
	Reflective Essay	✔	1	Writ 1.4	3
Per. 6 - Spanish II	International Exchange	✔	3	Speak 1.3	3
				List 1.1	4

Badge	Listening / Speaking	Writing	Mathematics	Science	Social Studies	The Arts
Entries / Required	2 / 2	6 / 8	3 / 6	1 / 3	3 / 4	2 / 4

Source: Copyright © 2018 Ideas Consulting, Inc. Used with permission.

The second part of the report shows the progress toward the badges. The reviewers can see the list of badges required for graduation and see the student's progress toward each.

The completeness page gives both the student and reviewer a sense of the breadth of work contained within the portfolio. Although for practical reasons the reviewers aren't going to look at all the entries, it is helpful to get an overall listing. It might prompt questions, such as "I see multiple entries from most of your classes, but only one from Spanish. Can you tell me more about that?"

What's important to note here is that the completeness page isn't an invitation to re-grade the work that's been submitted; the reviewers aren't expected to verify the scores done by other teachers any more than they are expected to verify the grades from other teachers on a student's report card. Just like the personal statement, the completeness page is designed to give the reviewers some more information about the student. In this case, it's a visual sense of what the student was able to accomplish this year.

The process of reviewing the tour is also an opportunity to talk about exceptions with the student. Perhaps the student is a transfer and didn't have an opportunity to complete as many tasks as others; perhaps there's some other explanation for why the student's entries may be higher or lower than typical. Rather than guessing, it's worth actually talking to the student about any such discrepancy.

The fourth prompt in the Action Plan tour asks students to review their work and provide some insight into their plans. The **action plan** section asks the student to consider what's missing from the completeness page and to identify, specifically, how they can fill in the missing gaps before graduation. How will they complete the rest of the badges?

Students can fill in many of the gaps with classes they will take in subsequent years. But if there are areas where a student has been struggling, this may need a deeper conversation. If the student has had difficulty with the problem-solving requirements up to this point, just having more opportunities to fulfill the requirements may not be enough.

Issues like that are what make the tour process useful. There can be a celebratory aspect to the process, with students basking in the glow of their accomplishments—and enabling such recognition is a great thing. At the same time, this is a rare opportunity for students to talk about their overall work and about overall strategies for improvement. This setting, where we're looking at the work as a whole, isn't focused on one class or one assignment; it's taking a step back to look at the larger picture. What can we do to help students complete the badges? To achieve their goals? To be truly successful with their action plans? The student isn't just presenting the action plan; the student is looking for *feedback* on that plan.

Mt. Hope's version of the **best work** prompt asks students to think about two of the school's key areas (communication and problem solving) and to select a sample entry for each. At this point, they reflect on the work using the reflection prompt we saw earlier in the chapter.

Finally, the student is asked to discuss **work related to my interests and goals**. Here, the student is connecting the work to a larger goal beyond those required by the school.

The Growth over Time Tour

The Action Plan tour is helpful while students are working toward fulfilling their requirements. When students have completed all the badges, they can do a variation called a Growth over Time tour as developed by Mt. Hope High School.

1. Cover/personal statement
2. Requirements summary (a report showing all the entries added to the portfolio this year)
3. Growth over time
4. My strengths
5. My area of interest
6. Future planning

Here, the action plan and best work sections are replaced by variations called growth over time and my strengths. The action plan section isn't needed because the student has fulfilled the requirements.

The **growth over time** prompt asks students to consider how they got to this point. The student is asked to select two entries—one entry that was not proficient and a second one that was proficient. What is the difference between these two entries? The student is asked to think about what has changed. To help guide the reflection, they can consider the following questions:

- Describe the artifact from the assignment that *was* **proficient**. How does the proficient artifact reflect your growth/improvement in this skill area?

- Describe the artifact from the assignment that was *not* **proficient**. How does it show your struggle in this area?.

- What strategies did you use to improve/grow in this area?

- You need to be specific.... [For example], what part of the writing do you find difficult (i.e., thesis, evidence to support your thinking, analysis)?

Schools often talk about wanting students to be lifelong learners. In this exercise, students are given the opportunity to show what that looks like. By thinking about something that was a struggle—and figuring out what is different—students consider their own process of learning.

Similarly, the section on **my strengths** asks students to consider the skills in which they excel. Many students are able to complete this tour during the end of junior year; asking students to articulate their strengths can be helpful as they write job applications and college admissions essays.

The growth over time tour becomes more of a "where do we go from here" conversation than the action plan tour. Completing the required badges is a big deal and should be celebrated as such; it's also an opportunity to consider what's going to come next.

Sample Tours at Three Grade Levels

Let's consider another variation. At Ponaganset High School, students present their work at the end of each year in grades 9, 10, and 11, with the tour varying a bit from year to year. (See Figures A.13–A.16 in the Appendix for more complete samples of these tours and accompanying rubrics.)

Grade 9 Tour

Cover

1. Are you on track?
2. Your growth as a learner
   - Choose one entry that shows your growth as a learner.
3. Ponaganset Graduation Expectation (PGE) strength/need: Academic goal setting
   - From the list of required expectations, select one you think is a strength.
   - From the list of required expectations, select one in which you need to improve.
   - Set an academic goal for the coming year.

4. Life after high school: Career goal setting

- What are your plans for after high school?

- What is your career goal? What steps can you take in the next year to reach it?

5. Résumé

6. Advice to a new 9th grader

Ponaganset's version of the requirements/completeness page is called **are you on track?** This school has quantified how many entries a student should have in the portfolio each year to be on track to graduate. In fact, the school has set up milestones throughout the year, letting students know where they're expected to be each term. Along with the report, however, students are asked to respond to a prompt that asks them whether they're on track and, if not, what plans they're going to make to get back on track in the next year.

The second item, **growth as a learner**, is similar to what we saw in Mt. Hope's growth over time tour, but in this case, 9th graders only need to select one entry.

Items 3 and 4 are meant to merge the end-of-year review with the student's individual learning plan. In the **strength/need** section, the student is asked to look at the work in the portfolio and determine which badges represent areas of strength and which are in need of improvement. What's interesting here is that the student is also asked to think about an academic goal for next year. Instead of just having students meet with a guidance counselor, the school takes advantage of this moment when students are reflecting anyway, asking them to identify a goal they want to achieve. This should stem directly from students' thoughts on their areas of strength and need.

Similarly, the students are asked to share their thoughts about **life after high school**. At the end of 9th grade, these can be vague, and that's OK, but the question does encourage the student to look at some area for consideration. These early conversations help students understand something about the fields they are interested in. For example, if a student wants to be a nurse, that student needs to plan for attending college.

The **résumé** section was not in Ponaganset's original tour. Dave Moscarelli, the school's portfolio coordinator (and the state's 2015 Teacher of the Year) tells the story of how one teacher was helping a 12th grade student prepare a résumé for a scholarship application. The student hadn't been asked to do one before and was in a bit of a panic. After asking around, Mr. Moscarelli found other students were experiencing the same issue, and so, the résumé became part of the 12th grade tour. Later, students brought up the fact that putting together a résumé in senior year was tricky because they couldn't remember all the things they had done throughout their four years. They asked, "Could you make us do a résumé every year?" From then on, the résumé became a part of the 9th, 10th, and 11th grade tours as well.

Now the résumé for a typical 14-year-old is not going to be very deep. But again, the tour is a chance to practice habits, and documenting key activities from the year has proven quite helpful to students.

The final section, **advice to a new 9th grader**, calls for a different type of reflection. It's another way to get students to reflect on their work, not just by thinking about themselves, but by explaining the experience to another student.

The 10th Grade Tour

Cover

1. Are you on track?

2. Growth as a learner

   • Compare and contrast two entries that show your growth as a learner.

3. Ponaganset Graduation Expectation (PGE) strength/need: Academic goal setting

   • What area did you identify as needing improvement last year?

   • Now that it's a year later, what progress have you made?

   • Set an academic goal for the coming year.

4. Life after high school: Career goal setting

   • What plans did you set last year? Are your goals still the same?

   • Complete a career inventory.

   • What is your career goal now? What steps can you take in the next year to reach it?

5. Résumé

   • Feel free to update last year's résumé.

The 10th grade tour has the same sections as the 9th grade tour, minus the last item about advice to a new 9th grader. However, the prompts in the sections are different. Students are now asked to go back to their 9th grade tours and consider the goals they set, as well as their areas of strength and need. The prompts ask them to think about their work a little more deeply to see whether they're on the same page. But in this tour, the focus is on determining the students' insights about their own academic and career goals and how their work both informs those goals and helps them figure out where they need to do more work.

The 11th Grade Tour

The 11th grade tour has the same sections as the 10th grade tour, plus two more. Students are asked to talk about their community service activities, and they're also asked to think about potential ideas for their senior exhibition, an independent project that they need to complete for graduation. The common sections, though, ask students to think about their areas of strength and need and to review the work from the past three years.

Both Mt. Hope and Ponaganset have rubrics for the end-of-year reviews. We'll look more closely at end-of-year rubrics later in the chapter.

The Subject-Area Tour

The subject-area tour is particularly useful for students who want to demonstrate a number of different skills within a specific discipline. For example, students can use tours to show their best work in the arts. Figure 5.4 shows one school's requirements for the visual arts tour.

The key idea here is that students can build this tour over time. They can begin the tour with their first course in high school, seeing all of the requirements right from the start. Perhaps the first-year course focuses on drawing, which would address several of the requirements. The student won't be able to take a course on sculpture or modeling until a later year—and only then would the student need to complete the requirement for the three-dimensional artwork. The tour is set up as a multiyear (or at least multicourse) process. It's meant to be a challenge, but it's also meant to ensure that students will have a variety of artifacts that demonstrate what the school defines as the crucial components of an arts portfolio.

A subject-area tour can focus on growth over time. To do this, the tour might ask the student to select a similar piece at certain set points of the year for purposes of comparison. In language arts, the tour might include an oral presentation from the second and fourth quarters of each year; the tour could ask the student to comment on any improvements since the last presentation and what the student wants to work on next. Similarly, in music or theater, the tour might include an entry looking at each big event, such as a reflection after each chorus concert. Or it might chronicle a single event in depth, such as including a student's weekly journal that documents how the student prepared for a play or musical and how he or she may have revised their notions about the character they're playing. In physical education, regular events can be tracked, from charting the time to complete one lap of the track to recording the components of the Presidential Youth Fitness Program. Here, the tour will have a collection of artifacts; the reflection should comment on the changes over time.

FIGURE 5.4 | **High School Visual Arts Portfolio**

Creating
From the list of entries, please select a minimum of six original artworks that meet the following criteria:
- Two must be drawings
  **One from observation
  **One other drawing
- At least one three-dimensional artwork
- At least two artworks that show effective use of color
- At least one artwork that shows influence or understanding of cultural, social, or historical contexts
- At least one artwork that uses concepts or content from other subjects
- All must effectively use the elements and principles of art
- At least two must communicate intent
- The portfolio must include a variety of at least three different processes and materials:
  **Drawing
  **Printmaking
  **Painting
  **Photography
  **Digital arts
  **Ceramics
  **Sculpture

Source: Mt. Hope High School, Bristol-Warren Regional School District, Rhode Island. Used with permission.

The Quest/Project Tour

The tours for a project or quest can be a record of the student's journey to completing the project. There can be multiple milestones in any project, as we saw with the samples in Chapter 3. In a tour, the student can upload each piece as it gets completed, from the initial concept through the final presentation.

The components of a project tour should let us see the *process* as well as the *product*. A reviewer should be able to see where things changed along the way and how the student handled any obstacles that emerged. Even when projects go smoothly, the student typically needs to elaborate and revise the initial idea. For example, a student's plans to write a play or create a mobile app might prove to be too ambitious; part of the way through the project, the student might decide to complete one act or focus on a subset of the app's features. Through this tour, we gain insight into a student's thinking process and how the student adapts as needed.

The College Tour

One common question is "How do we use digital portfolios to help with college admissions?" There are definitely ways for portfolios to help, but a lot depends on the specific student and the specific college.

For College Readiness and Admissions

The landscape of college admissions is changing. More than 140 colleges have joined the Coalition for Access, Affordability, and Success. Starting with the admissions cycle in 2016–2017, the Coalition began offering new tools for college exploration and admissions. While students can use the "Coalition App" to gather the traditional data (background information, high school transcripts, recommendations, and so on), the Coalition also provides additional features.

What's new is that each student now has an online area called a *virtual locker*—essentially, a digital portfolio. In this space, students can upload their best work. This is the student's private space, and it is only visible to the people the student wants to open it up to. However, there are accounts available for teachers, counselors, mentors, parents, or anyone else who wants to help the student.

The contents of the locker are not automatically available to the colleges. When it comes to the actual admissions process, each of the individual colleges will determine what (if anything) students can submit from their lockers. The artifacts that students ultimately submit should make the argument that this student is ready and able to meet the demands of the college's curriculum.

Now let's be realistic; if a college has 30,000 students applying for 3,000 slots, the admissions staff isn't going to pore over a half dozen entries for every single student. Any tour prepared for an admissions officer needs to take no more than 60 to 90 seconds. That's probably just enough time to talk about one or possibly two entries.

So, what should students include? Here are some possibilities, which we will look at one by one.

- Their ability to work independently.
- Their preparation for the major they wish to pursue.
- How this college will help you achieve their goals.
- Something interesting about them that wouldn't appear elsewhere.

An entry that shows their ability to work independently. Colleges value students who can show their independence in two ways. First, it helps to know that students can pursue topics of their own choosing, projects that arose from their personal interests. Second, it helps to show that the student can be self-organized. It's one thing to have an idea; it's another to put in the effort and see the project through. Projects don't have to turn out perfectly; in fact, showing the resilience required to overcome difficulties is valuable.

Here's one example. One student was interested in environmental issues, particularly in the wake of the Deepwater Horizon oil spill off the coast of Louisiana. The student organized a team to go to New Orleans and thought she had made arrangements to do volunteer work. On arrival, however, she learned that the volunteer group had no record of her or her team. Rather than give up, she regrouped and found another volunteer organization working on a different type of environmental cleanup. The project didn't go as planned, but the student showed the ability to deliver an appropriate experience for her team.

An entry that shows their preparation for the major they wish to pursue. Some students are certain about what they'll study in college; others are not. However, a college tour should show that they're at least prepared to start examining their options. If they're interested in doing something in health care, they can show that they've gained some background in science or caretaking skills. If they have only a general idea—"something in the arts"— they can show that they have some background to build on.

An entry that shows how this college will help them achieve their goals. Why are they interested in applying to this particular college? How will their experience there differ from their experience anywhere else? For example, if they know that a college is known for its pioneering work in computer graphics, they may want to include a sample that shows their interest in animation or data visualization.

An entry that tells something interesting about them that wouldn't appear elsewhere. The application shows grades and primary activities. But it may not show students' other skills; maybe they help keep their household organized or help take care of elderly relatives. There may be some under-the-radar things that they do that demonstrate habits such as resilience or perseverance. Elaborating on those skills in the admissions tour can provide more insight into your readiness for college.

For Placement

A college tour may also be useful for placement. That is, students can prepare a set of entries not just for getting into college, but for determining what courses may be most appropriate for them to take.

Sometimes this can work well in technical or performance areas where test scores aren't obvious. For example, a student interested in a communications degree could put together a tour showing her work with video. An online "demo reel" could highlight different styles of video production (a news report, commercial, music video, business presentation, etc.) and help determine whether a student might be able to skip over "Video Production 101" and go into a more advanced course.

A college tour can also be a supplement for students who may struggle with test scores. Colleges are relying less on tests for various parts of the admissions and placement processes. For example, in 2017, the California State University system announced that it would not rely on test scores to determine whether students are required to take remedial classes; rather, the university wants to rely more on "previous classroom performance and other measures" (Xia, 2017). A tour that shows the student's skills—and the specific areas where the student struggles—can help both the student and the university determine what supports would be most appropriate.

Protocols for Presenting

So, once these tours are in place, what do we do with them?

As mentioned in Chapter 4, feedback is crucial to a portfolio system's acceptance. If students put serious effort into assembling and reflecting on a portfolio and then just get a "check-plus" at the end, they will most likely feel that their efforts haven't been rewarded. Portfolios *can* become just one more thing to do. But if you want to unlock the power of the portfolios, some type of review is necessary.

Portfolio reviews can start simply. For example, a portfolio for a writing badge can be submitted as part of an English class. The teacher doing the reviewing, however, needs to be able to provide specific feedback to the student; what does the teacher see in the body of work that is truly worth commenting on?

Student-led conferences are another way to go. For many schools, the structure is already in place, and the schedules are set for the conferences. By drawing the portfolio into the conference structure, students can engage in conversation about what they have done well, where they need to improve, and what they would like to learn more about. It isn't just listening to the student present; it's about the deeper dialogue concerning where the student should focus next.

Because end-of-year reviews often involve multiple teachers, one simple way to start is to have teachers pair up; if you have an advisory system at your school, then two advisories can get together. The teacher teams could ask students to prepare a tour and then do 10-minute interviews with each student in turn. It might take a few sessions (depending on how often your advisories meet and for how long), but it can provide a way for each student to get some personalized feedback from multiple sources.

The end-of-year reviews described in this chapter are a little more elaborate and have become something of a ritual at their schools. At both Mt. Hope and Ponaganset high schools, the teacher pairs usually come from different departments or include an administrator or a counselor paired with a classroom teacher. Many special needs students are scheduled with their primary teacher or case worker. At both schools, the teacher time is freed up by releasing the rest of the students. For example, at Ponaganset, the reviews are scheduled during the exam period, when students are not required to be on campus unless they have a scheduled exam.

Here's the usual protocol: First, students present their tour for about 10 minutes, describing the selected entries and walking through their responses to the various prompts. The teachers have access to the tours ahead of time and may have already read the reflections. After the presentation, the teachers ask the student some specific questions about the work and the student's future plans. This can be a casual discussion or a formal presentation; that's up to the school. Often, parents are invited to sit in on the session.

After the presentation and question-and-answer period, the student leaves and the teachers get together. They will review the rubric for the tour and come up with a common score.

It's worth reminding that the tour evaluation does *not* mean that the student's work is being reevaluated. This isn't about going back and checking the student's grade on this math project or that health entry. Rather, the rubric corresponds to the sections of the tour. Figure 5.5 shows a sample end-of-year rubric.

This rubric is primarily focused on the quality of the reflection. It asks the student to identify learned skills and knowledge and explain how he or she will respond to identified areas of weakness; it requests the student's thoughts on the year's successes and failures, and it asks the student to explain how his or her advice for an incoming 9th grader will improve that student's success. So even though they may not be doing well in all of their classes, students can pass the rubric *if* they're able to articulate what's going wrong and the next steps they might take.

How much does this portfolio rubric count? It depends. In Rhode Island, starting with the graduating class of 2008, students have been required to demonstrate proficiency in six areas (math, science, English, social studies, technology, and the arts) through at least two performance-based activities. Many schools choose a portfolio to address one of those two requirements, so passing the rubric ultimately means that the student can graduate.

The assessment can be weighted in other ways. At Ponaganset, for example, the rubric is translated into a grade and that grade is used as 10 percent of the final exam grade in every class. (Note that it's the final *exam* grade in question, not the overall final course grade. The final exam represents about 20 percent of the overall final grade, so the portfolio represents 10 percent of that 20 percent.)

Narragansett High School reviews its senior project tours in a similar way. On a designated day, the 9th, 10th, and 11th grade students are dismissed early. The seniors present their projects to a panel, which includes both teachers and community members. These outside reviewers come into the school early and are able to look at the students' project tours before the start of the session; they will typically review four or five students that day. They note the student's progress from the first sign of commitment to the end of the research paper.

FIGURE 5.5 | **End-of-Year Tour Rubric, 9th Grade**

"Weight" indicates the multiplier for that row. For example, if a student scores an "Advanced" (4) on the first row, which has a weight of 8, the student receives 32 total points for this row of the rubric. In this rubric, the maximum number of points is 100.

"Prorated" means that the student has not been in attendance for the full year at this school.

	4	3	2	1	0	SCORE
1a. On Track to Graduate Weight: 8	Portfolio is on track with 8 acceptable entries *or* 1 entry for 100% of classes taken (if prorated)	Portfolio is not on track with 7 acceptable entries *or* 1 entry for approx. 85% of classes taken (if prorated)	Portfolio is not on track with 6 acceptable entries *or* 1 entry for approx. 75% of classes taken (if prorated)	Portfolio is not on track with 4–5 acceptable entries *or* 1 entry for approx. 50–65% of classes taken (if prorated)	0–3 entries *or* entries for < 50% of classes	
1b. Steps for Improvement (only for students who are not on track) Weight: 0	Identifies areas for improvement and provides detailed steps for improving work in the future	Identifies areas for improvement and provides steps for the future	Identifies areas of improvement, but steps for improvement are incomplete or do not make sense	No clear delineation of steps for improvement	No attempt	
2. Growth as a Learner Weight: 3	In-depth and insightful reflection that includes -clear identification of learned skills and knowledge	Good reflection on the work that includes -identification of learned skills and knowledge	Basic reflection on the work, where there is a genuine attempt to -identify learned skills and knowledge	Reflection is largely incomplete; a poor attempt.	No attempt	

2. Growth as a Learner Weight: 3—*(continued)*	-substantive discussion of the challenge the entry provided includes supporting examples	- discussion of the challenge the entry provided	-discuss the challenge the entry provides However, some of the reflection is unclear or incomplete	
3. Ponagan-set Graduation Expectation (PGE) Strength and Need Weight: 5	Student clearly identifies one PGE that is an area of strength and one PGE that is an area of weakness. Creates an in-depth and insightful reflection that discusses why these PGEs were chosen and how the student will respond to the identified area of weakness Identifies and explains current academic goal with in-depth plan to meet goal	Student clearly identifies one PGE that is an area of strength and one PGE that is an area of weakness. Creates an in-depth reflection that discusses why these PGEs were chosen and how the student will respond to the identified area of weakness Identifies and explains current academic goal with plan to meet goal	Student clearly identifies one PGE that is an area of strength and one PGE that is an area of weakness. Creates an adequate reflection that discusses why these PGEs were chosen and how the student will respond to the identified area of weakness	Student fails to clearly identify one PGE that is an area of strength and one that is an area of weakness. Fails to effectively reflect on why these PGEs were chosen Failure to identify current academic goal *and/or* No evidence of plans to improve PGE weakness and meet academic goals

(continued)

FIGURE 5.5 | **End-of-Year Tour Rubric, 9th Grade**—*(continued)*

	4	3	2	1	0	SCORE
3. Ponagan-set Graduation Expectation (PGE) Strength and Need Weight: 5 *—(continued)*			Identifies and explains current academic goal with little evidence of a plan to meet goal *or* Student clearly identifies only one PGE that is an area of strength or weakness. Creates an in-depth reflection that discusses why this PGE was chosen and how the student will respond to the identified area of weakness. Identifies and explains current academic goal with little evidence of a plan to meet goal.			

Tours: Student Presentations of Portfolios • 123

4. Life After High School **Weight: 4**	Student effectively responds to all aspects of the prompt and supports responses with details and/or examples.	Student effectively responds to the following aspects of the prompt: - identification of top work values from Career Cluster Survey - identification of careers of most interest and career goal - identification of current/future courses aligned to career goal -identification of resources that may be used to meet goal	Student effectively responds to three aspects of the prompt.	Student effectively responds to one or two aspects of the prompt. The overall response is largely incomplete.	No attempt
5. Résumé **Weight: 1**	Student's résumé is uploaded. -student effectively states and explains plans for improving résumé	Student's résumé is uploaded. -student effectively states plans for improving résumé	Student's résumé is uploaded. -student makes a poor attempt to state ways to improve résumé	Student's résumé is uploaded. -student makes no attempt to state ways to improve résumé	No attempt

(continued)

FIGURE 5.5　|　**End-of-Year Tour Rubric, 9th Grade—(continued)**

	4	3	2	1	0	SCORE
6. Advice to a New 9th Grader Weight: 1	In-depth and insightful reflection on success or failure this year. Includes -explicit and clear identification of one piece of advice -well-developed explanation of how the advice will improve the new 9th grader's success	Good reflection on success or fail-ure this year and includes - identification of one piece of advice - explanation of how the advice will improve the new 9th grader's success	Basic reflection on success or failure this year. Inconsis-tent but genuine attempt to -identify one piece of advice -explain how the advice will improve the new 9th grader's success	Reflection is largely incomplete; a poor attempt	No attempt	
Oral Communication Weight: 2	Delivery (including eye contact, speak-ing voice, posture, and gestures) is natural, comfortable, and appropriate. Quality of delivery adds to presenta-tion's effectiveness.	Delivery is natural, comfortable, and appropriate. Delivery is consistent.	Delivery is inconsis-tent, and elements may be distracting at times.	Delivery is highly distracting or dis-ruptive, decreasing effectiveness of presentation.	No attempt	

RF (Reflecting on Performance) Weight: 1					No attempt
	Includes well-chosen and specific facts and details relevant to the controlling idea to create depth of reflection	Includes sufficient facts and details to effectively support the main points of the reflection	Includes facts and details relevant to the purpose or the main focus	Includes irrelevant facts to the purpose or main idea	
	Applies sophisticated organizational structures within paragraphs / oral comments that enhance the progression of ideas	Applies organizational structures within paragraphs / oral comments that support a progression of ideas	Applies some organizational structures within paragraphs / oral comments that allows for a progression of ideas	Applies few organizational structures that allows for a progression of ideas	
	Uses precise and descriptive language which clarifies and supports the reflection	Uses language which clarifies and supports intent by questioning, comparing, connecting, interpreting, or analyzing	Uses language which partially supports intent	Uses language which does not support intent	
	Skillfully applies the rules and mechanics of writing / speaking: making no errors	Consistently applies the rules and mechanics of writing/speaking (e.g., punctuation, spelling, word usage) making unobtrusive errors	Applies the rules and mechanics of writing: making occasional obtrusive errors	Inconsistently applies the rules and mechanics of writing / speaking: making repetitive errors	
					TOTAL SCORE:

Source: Ponaganset High School, Foster-Glocester Regional School District, Rhode Island. Used with permission.

Having been assured that all the panelists have read the material, the students can begin their presentations. They usually dress up for the occasion. Some have props for their demonstrations, such as the student who built a robot; another student brought the panel outside to show what she had learned about archery.

Each student presents for approximately 15 minutes and then stands for questions from the group. Afterward, the panelists thank the student and ask him or her to wait outside while they discuss the student work and come up with a single score for the rubric. At that point, the student comes back in and together they discuss the assessment.

What's interesting is the dynamic here; we have teachers who know the students and community members who may not have been in a school in many years. In this case, the clarity of the rubric is crucial because it ensures that the panelists are looking for the same thing. At the same time, it's useful to have both "warm" and "cool" perspectives (McDonald, 1992). The people who know the student personally can speak to the student's overall skills and growth; the people who do not know the student can refer to the specific text and artifacts that have been provided.

The presentation often represents the culmination of a term, a year, or even a student's entire school career, or it may just be a subset of the student's achievements. In either case, in the process of collecting, selecting, reflecting on, and presenting the work, the connection between the student and the school comes into focus.

And how do students experience these presentations? They often say that the presentations are nerve-racking, but that they allow them to discuss who they are in ways that don't normally occur during the school year. Teachers regularly comment on how they learn something new about each of the students who presents—even if they have had that student in class all year. Allowing each student to have time in their individual spotlight may be particularly useful to the "average" student. Creating tours and allowing students to talk about who they are as individual learners enables those students to shine in their personal accomplishments. It's a step toward ensuring, as Deborah Meier (2002) has pointed out, that no child remains anonymous.

Creating a Badge- and Portfolio-Friendly School Culture

How do we make sure the badges and portfolios are valued?

How do we build on what we already have?

What else has to change?

When we learn about the human body, we usually break it down into various systems: the circulatory system, the skeletal system, the digestive system, the nervous system, and so on. We can study each of these systems in turn, and, for the purposes of an introductory study, this is a perfectly reasonable way to start.

But we know the human body is more complex than that. Take in too many of the wrong foods, and we can increase the cholesterol in the bloodstream; clearly, the digestive and circulatory systems respond to each other. In medicine, treating a symptom in one area can have side effects that affect some other part of the body. The fact is, the body's systems interact with one another, and a change to one can have an effect on many others.

Schools have their own complexity. Any teacher will tell you that the classroom dynamics of any group of 15, 25, or 35 students will change as quickly as the weather. Multiply that by the dozens of classrooms in the building; add in the relationships with parents, administrators, and the community; and set this all in a backdrop of changing state regulations—it's no wonder we have no simple, single formula to approach the issue of school change.

Yet many school initiatives are predicated on the promise of a simple solution. Whether it's adding technology, changing the schedule, or grouping students differently, there's this ongoing hope that one change will transform the whole school.

Digital badges and portfolios are exciting, useful tools that can be helpful to teachers and students. However, they aren't implemented in a vacuum. To be effective, a digital badge and portfolio initiative needs to fit your circumstances and be accompanied by another essential question: "What else has to change?"

Setting a Purpose

Schools should be *learning organizations*. This term, coined by Peter Senge, an influential professor of management and organizational strategy, doesn't just refer to the fact that students learn in schools; in a learning organization, *everyone* in the school community is working toward both "individual and collective aspirations" (Senge, Cambron-McCabe, Lucas, Smith, Dutton, & Kleiner, 2012).

Among the tenets of a learning organization is the *shared vision*. This is not a top-down or bottom-up approach to change; a shared vision is a common understanding of what we want our school to be like *and* an individual understanding of what I need to do to help achieve that vision. It should dovetail with the notion of *personal mastery*, meaning that each person understands what he or she wants to achieve, that each one has a realistic assessment of his or her current skills. An organization that values personal mastery *and* has a shared vision will be able to tackle innovative practices.

When it comes to implementing digital badges and portfolios, the first question we need to ask is, What is our purpose for taking this on? A common mistake with many initiatives is to confuse implementation with goals. For example, when schools move to add technology, the wrong goal is "We will have X percentage of students go online" or "Students will spend Y hours in the environment." The *right* goal is "Students will engage with the material in a different way" or "We will help students better understand concepts where they struggled previously."

Similarly, the purpose here is not just to create a set of student portfolios. The purpose is to use those portfolios toward some larger educational goal. There are some purposes that work well—and some that don't.

Purposes That Work Well

Improving Our Understanding of Standards and Mastery

When standards-based learning was originally introduced, many teachers were encouraged to write the standards on the board or post them prominently in the classroom. The standards, however, were essentially inert; they were in the front of the room but quickly faded into the background as students and teachers focused on the current lesson.

Digital portfolios and badges require a higher level of interaction with standards (or competencies, proficiencies, or whatever your school calls them). When teachers determine assignments that are portfolio-worthy, they're indicating that the current task is closely aligned with certain standards. Similarly, when students submit their work or create a tour, they have to think about what kind of evidence best demonstrates a certain standard—which, in turn, implies that the student has actually understood the standard.

Portfolios can accompany the introduction of common rubrics. Through tour presentations, students will be presenting tasks from multiple classes. The common rubrics can help teachers as they look at the work going on in other parts of the school. These common rubrics start to create a common language and, ultimately, a common understanding of what it means to master a standard in, say, persuasive writing.

Personalizing Instruction

Personalization is a hot topic; every school, state, and district seems to be promoting its efforts to personalize education. Still, it's not clear that everyone is approaching this in the same way. It's worth asking, What does *personalization* mean to our school or district?

The State of Rhode Island's Office of Innovation (2016) has looked at how 10 different organizations, from the U.S. Department of Education to the Gates Foundation, have defined personalization, and it has found that certain key phrases appear throughout the definitions, including

- Competency-based progression
- Meets individual student needs

- Standards-aligned
- Student interests
- Student ownership
- Socially embedded
- Formative assessments
- Flexible learning environments

Each school needs to come to a decision about what aspects of personalization it has in mind. Just as important, schools need to think about whether their initiatives really meet their definitions of personalization. Many learning management systems claim that they can help schools personalize, but often the only part of the definition they're referring to is that students can go at their own pace. Students don't have much choice in how they interact with the material if the only thing they can control is how quickly or how slowly they can move through the lessons. The concepts of *student ownership* or *student interests* are low on the priority list.

Digital portfolios get to the key notions of personalization because they're the ultimate way for students to show how they meet standards. Every student in a school might have to demonstrate a common set of standards, but each student should be able to use the portfolio to display those standards in his or her own way.

Teachers are the crucial component in ensuring that digital badges and portfolios are being used to personalize the school environment. The concept of "meeting individual needs" is very different from a human perspective than from a computer's. Teachers who know their students well are the ones who can help a student see a problem from a different angle, make a different analogy, or connect today's issue with something the student has previously accomplished. Teachers understand student motivations, what's going on outside the classroom, and how the student is interacting within the school community. Thus, the conversations around a portfolio between teacher and student are going to inherently be richer than any computer-generated feedback.

There's a spectrum of personalization approaches that range from allowing students to select tasks from a teacher-approved list to allowing them to select any task they want, including tasks that take place outside school. In addition, to seriously address the idea of letting students pursue their own interests and take ownership, schools need to offer multiple opportunities for students to have a major hand in designing their own tasks and projects. Portfolios can be a great way for schools to transition into personalization; over time, the entries in a student's final tour might move from being all from teacher-designated assignments to including a majority of entries coming from the student-initiated tasks.

Promoting Deeper Communication Among Stakeholders

The potential of digital badges and portfolios is to provide a deeper conversation. An end-of-year review or a parent-teacher conference can be a chance for students, teachers, and parents to take a step back and review the student's overall progress. It can be powerful to see the student's growth over time; the patterns that emerge across entries can inform all parties about the types of tasks that most engage the student and that are of particular interest. The purpose of improving communication is to get to know students better. The ritual of an end-of-year review—and the different conversations that arise as a result—can be most insightful.

Fostering Reflection

A learning organization requires reflective thinking. The key component of reflection is that it be a conscious, deliberate effort. Reflection doesn't always have to be deep, but it does have to be intentional. What did I learn from this experience? What could I do differently? What worked well?

The process of assembling a portfolio provides multiple opportunities for reflection. A student can reflect briefly on each entry as it goes in; this allows the student to think about the work while it is still fresh. A tour is a chance to reflect on the body of work or look at the growth over time. Assembling a presentation for an audience, whether it consists of parents, community members, admissions officers, or employers, should encourage students to think about what skills that audience wants to see and what fresh insights the student has to offer.

Supporting New Assessment Methods and Types of Tasks

The use of portfolios and badges can support other initiatives. For example, a school that is introducing project-based learning can use the digital badges as a visual way of showing student progress. Implementing new projects can suggest a new type of curriculum and methodology in the classroom, but if they're tied to old checklist scoring methods, the ultimate value of the projects may be lost. On the other hand, if a student earns a badge for completing a project (or other assessment, such as an updated contemporary version of an old assignment), it shows that the innovation extends to all the teaching, learning, and assessment processes.

Purposes That Don't Work Well

Focusing on Technology

In some schools, the attraction of a digital portfolio is simply that students will have more reasons for going online. Perhaps the school has purchased new tablets or laptops and wants to see more return on that investment.

For many students, the idea of going online is hardly fresh—and it's not very sustaining as a purpose. Students may be willing to try all sorts of new software or apps, but, once the novelty wears off, the simple fact that the portfolio has moved from paper to digital is not inherently interesting.

However, a portfolio whose purpose is to show *how* students use technology is a different matter. Students could show how they use technology to conduct online research, write essays or create presentations, generate content to put on websites, or add music to a video production. If your school's goal is to improve the use of technology, it's not just the portfolio that will do it; it's the quality of the tasks that go into the portfolio that will help you achieve your goal.

The State/District Is Making Us Do It

Digital portfolios and badges can help schools meet certain mandates set out by a state or district, and certainly schools have an obligation to comply with the designated regulations. However, when the entire motivation for a school's involvement is based on compliance, any initiative will lose its power. We have seen schools approach a state requirement on portfolios by asking, "What's the absolute minimum that we need to do?" When a school, particularly its leadership, is simply going through the motions, teachers and students can tell and will respond accordingly.

When faced with a compliance issue, schools need to couple the state's requirement with something that teachers and students are actually looking for. What purposes from the previous section will motivate your teachers? Try presenting the initiative this way to faculty: "We know that too many of our students are falling through the cracks, and we want to get to understand them better. Badges and portfolios will help us do that—and, by the way, they will help us meet a state requirement." By doing so, school leaders can expect a different result than if the initiative is seen as just one more thing to do.

Building on What We Have

School leaders often ask, "How do we get buy-in?" Whether it be from teachers, students, parents, or other community members, the champions of the cause want to know how to move from "initiative" to a regular part of school life. As Michael Fullan (2015) has noted, such transitions can often take from 5 to 10 years. Of course, some transitions occur faster, whether schools want them to or not; advances in technology or ramifications from current events often require a more rapid response, such as how to handle issues that arise on social media.

Still, many classroom practices are resistant to change. Sarason (1996) noted that the "regularities" of schools—the familiar arrangement of one teacher with two or three dozen students in a classroom focusing on a single subject for a 45- to 60-minute period—are the hardest items to address. For example, rubrics are often commonplace, but many students, teachers, and parents look at a rubric and just ask, "How does this translate to a letter grade?"

An initiative like digital portfolios and badges usually requires a school-wide effort, and that will take a little while. Still, you can get the buy-in that will get you started and that will provide momentum. Four things are important here for school leaders to do.

Address a Need

Selecting a purpose that resonates with many of your faculty members is crucial. Any of the purposes we listed in the previous section—improving our understanding of standards and mastery, personalizing instruction, fostering reflection, encouraging deeper communication among stakeholders, and supporting new assessments—can be a reasonable purpose. The badges and portfolios may support some other initiative or need in your schools, such as a focus on literacy or math skills. What's important is that the faculty recognize the reason that they are being asked to do something different.

Start with Where Teachers Are Now

Beginning with digital portfolios can often mean that teachers are wrestling with two new concepts: the *digital* part and the *portfolio* part. To help deal with the unfamiliar, ground the work in something that *is* familiar. Ask teachers to consider a task they already assign that produces good evidence. Some teachers see examples of final products and assume that the portfolio has to contain elaborate quests and tasks. Assure teachers that they can ease into the work. The task they first select may be a relatively simple, but if it captures a moment of teaching and learning, and both students and teachers find the task worthwhile, that is probably a good place to start.

The goal for the first semester (or maybe even the first year) is just to go through the process. Students can add a couple of entries, which teachers can assess. Just to get started, all students might add the same entry. One school had the students simply type up their favorite (clean) joke in a document and then added that to the portfolio.

In later iterations, teachers can start altering the assignments or begin experimenting with formats (in terms of both technological formats and task formats) that are new to them. At that point, teachers can start to experiment with web video or podcasts or consider debates or skits where previously students gave straight presentations. To begin, though, it's best to keep it simple.

Start Small, but Let Everyone Know They Are Involved

Before bringing an entire school into an initiative, it's useful to have a pilot group check things out first. A small group of three to six teachers, representing different subject areas or grade levels, can work with their students to create a portfolio, perhaps with one or two entries from each class. This group can work out the logistics: how much time it takes to prepare the work, how to log into the accounts, how to handle makeup work. The pilot group doesn't have to be your most experienced or most tech-savvy teachers; in fact, one principal deliberately asked a tech-challenged teacher to participate, knowing that when that teacher succeeded, the rest of the faculty would say, "If Kathy can do it, I'm sure I can, too."

While the pilot group is doing its work, the rest of the faculty can be engaged. There may be parallel professional development that focuses on reviewing tasks or doing calibration exercises with rubrics. If teachers feel they're a part of shaping the initiative, they're more likely to respond well. A single teacher's suggestion might be relatively small; for example, at one school, a teacher wanted a button on the software to appear on the left, rather than on the right side of the screen. Honoring such requests goes a long way toward making the initiative feel like a collaborative effort.

The school leadership needs to make it clear that after the pilot group is done, there will be a rollout to the rest of the faculty. This rollout may be gradual. Many schools add a grade each year; they might start with grade 6 one year, adding grade 7 the next, and grade 8 the year after that. Still, teachers should know up front that they will be getting involved at some point, and their participation in task or rubric activities will be important in shaping the overall project.

Celebrate the Small Victories

The school leadership should routinely celebrate accomplishments as the project is getting implemented. Ideally, this should take place in some face-to-face setting, like a faculty meeting, rather than just in a memo. Recognizing that teachers have worked together to define a specific badge or calibrate a particular rubric or figured out the best way to logistically handle the use of cell phones in class for video shows that they are contributing to the overall initiative. When the principal recognizes such accomplishments—even when they're not perfect—it validates the effort.

Rituals That Support a Portfolio Initiative

Schools have many rituals. There are daily events, such as making morning announcements, lining up for recess, and navigating the cafeteria. And there are annual activities, such as photo day or the prom. Some principals stand in the hallway at the beginning of the day to greet students; others make an effort to engage with as many parents as possible. Faculty members will create their own rituals among themselves, from clarifying who is responsible for rinsing the coffee pots to how they celebrate birthdays.

Rituals can help establish digital badges and portfolios as a regular component of the school. At Ponaganset High School's end-of-year reviews, students sit down and walk through their tours with two teachers. To make this happen, time is set aside; the reviews are scheduled during the exam period. Rather than taking exams all day, the school has created a special schedule. On each of the designated days, the schedule is shortened and after lunch, the students *not* presenting go home. If there are three days of reviews, one-third of the students present each day. The change in the normal routine marks this as a special occasion for students.

For the faculty, this is something different as well. The teacher panels are set up so the teacher reviewers represent different departments. This means that teachers are often working with someone they don't typically spend much time with. The administrators in the school and district also participate, allowing some faculty to interact with educators from other parts of the district. In addition, the collaborative scoring everyone engages in is an opportunity for different kinds of interactions and to discuss what a "2" or a "3" means on the rubric.

The first year that Ponaganset conducted these reviews, the principal sent a note home, explaining the process. Although the letter was originally intended just to inform parents, the principal and faculty were pleased to learn that a number of parents came to the school and asked to watch their child's review. The next year, the school deliberately reached out to parents and invited them to come. The school set up some childcare services and added a spread of baked goods and drinks for the attending parents.

Other schools have created their own variations. In one school that had a strong advisory system, two advisory classrooms would get together. Together, the two advisory teachers would do the reviews for all the students in both classes. At another school, the local parent/teacher organization helped organize the event, setting up lunch and snacks and taking photos of students as they celebrated completing their portfolios.

One important part of the ritual is attaching stakes to make the reviews count. In one school we discussed, the portfolio presentation counted for 10 percent of the final exam grade. Other schools require the portfolio to be complete so the student is eligible to begin a capstone project or to participate in an out-of-school activity such as an apprenticeship.

You may have your own variation on these rituals. You could set up badge ceremonies that celebrate when students achieve a certain level; you could organize a "portfolio fair," structured like a science fair, where students show off their portfolios in booths for faculty, students, and community members. Some schools engage younger students by having them sit in on older students' presentations. The kinds of conversations you wish to engage in should help you shape the ritual to fit your needs.

Probably the most important part of the ritual, though, is that every student has a chance to be heard. Presenting one's body of work is different from the experience of turning in one assignment at a time. This makes the interaction with the panel even more important; the panel is looking at the student as a whole and giving feedback on an overall body of work. Providing an environment in which you're having an honest discussion and feedback on where the student needs to go is probably the most important component of any portfolio process, and the ritual that goes around it should help underline that fact.

Individual Learning Plans/Student Success Plans

When schools talk about the advantages of portfolios and badges for students, the focus is often on external audiences: "You'll want to show this to your graduation panel/college admissions officer/future employer!" All of this is definitely true. Perhaps, though, some students will be motivated by looking at an *internal* audience—that is, by asking "How can this be helpful to *me*?"

Many schools, particularly at the middle and high school level, ask students to create individual learning plans (ILP), also known as student success plans. The ILP is different from the individual education plans used for special education; it's designed for all students to do some backward planning of their own. Specifically, an ILP often asks a student to set goals in three areas: academic, career/college, and personal/social.

The problem in many schools, however, is that the goal setting ends there. The student writes down the goals, an advisor or a counselor looks at them, and that's the end of that until next year. Another more effective approach is to ask students to lay out steps toward achieving those goals—and those steps can be defined as a set of badges.

For example, a school could have a "college readiness" badge. To earn the badge, the student could take a number of specific steps, as shown in Figure 6.1.

The specifics of the badge requirements can vary, depending on your setting; the point is that these badges offer concrete steps for students to achieve. Thus, the learning plan could lend itself to a table like the one shown in Figure 6.2.

Many of the badges in the learning plan should overlap with the badges the student will earn in classes or through the existing structures of the school. The data for the attendance badge, for example, can come straight from the school's student information system. In other words, the learning plan does not have to be a compilation of entirely new activities; rather, it's a way to guide students to use the existing resources of the school more effectively. By providing deadlines and a visual cue to overall student progress, students, advisors, and counselors can more easily keep each student's individual goals front and center.

FIGURE 6.1 | **College Badge Readiness Requirements**

Academic Preparation	Requirements: • Make list of potential majors • Determine high school courses that lead toward those majors
Financial Preparation	• Create FAFSA account • Apply for scholarships
Application Process	• Determine colleges that offer your potential major • Create a Coalition app/Common app account • Maintain a résumé/activity list • Sign up for SAT/ACT • Find out deadlines for application
Social/Work Habit Readiness	• Participate in extracurricular activities (in or out of school) • Show how you manage time by showing your attendance record • Document ways you help in school/at home/in your community

Reporting Progress

Digital badges and portfolios provide a wealth of information about each student. The students can see what they have achieved and can link to the evidence that underlies those achievements. Tours can provide a walkthrough of the entries that are useful for a particular audience.

Even with all the information online, it's often helpful to have a summary page that provides an overview. Figure 6.3 shows an example of such a report.

The summary lists all of the required badges in the first column. The second column indicates the number of requirements the student needs to achieve. The third and fourth columns indicate this particular student's progress. We can see that the student has made progress on all of the badges listed. To earn the Arts badge, the student has opted to complete the Music badge. Even though there is nothing listed for Visual Arts or Dance, the student's Arts badge still counts as complete.

FIGURE 6.2 | **The Learning Plan: Fulfilling the Badge Requirements**

MY LEARNING PLAN			
Category	**Goal/Badge**	**Requirements I will complete**	**Deadline**
Academic	Improve my writing	• Practice in a weekly journal • Tutorials • Complete the English 9 writing badge	January 15
Career/College	College Readiness	• List potential majors • Make course plan for next three years • Record my activities	February 10
Personal/Social	Attendance	• No more than one late day	November 30
	Leadership	• Lead a project for the Entrepreneur club	June 30

The badge report can also have an "additional" section. This can list the badges the student is working on that go beyond the required elements. This way, a reader of the report can see the individual interests of this student. (The list of badges in this section can come straight out of the badges selected for the individual learning plan.)

A badge summary report can supplement the typical report card. The list of required badges shown on the left helps schools indicate what they value in all of their students; it separates a student's progress from individual classes or years and focuses instead on the goal itself. A look at this report doesn't lend itself to thinking about quarter averages or improving the student's GPA; rather, it encourages thinking about the overall set of requirements and what the student needs to do to meet them. It tells a more complete story of a student's performance and progress.

FIGURE 6.3 | **Student Badge Report**

STUDENT BADGE REPORT			
Date: _____			
Badge	**Requirements**	**Completed**	**Comments**
Speaking	2	1	Impressive preparation for in-class debate
Writing	5	3	
Math	5	4	
Arts	Music: 3	3	Performed well at winter concert
	Visual Arts: 3	--	
	Dance: 3	--	
Additional	Entrepreneur: 3	3	Completed business plan

Teacher and Administrator Portfolios

This book has examined digital badges and portfolios for students. Yet this same process can be used by faculty and administrators. When New York State adopted a new evaluation system for both teachers and principals, one district experimented with having the adults create their own portfolios (Niguidula, 2015). The principals had a set of criteria, consisting of state and district standards. Each principal also had specific goals that he or she was going to meet during the year. At the end of each year, the principals documented the ways they had achieved each of these goals and put the work into a digital portfolio.

For example, one principal described a combined arts/science initiative at his elementary school. He had successfully applied for a grant to bring local artists into the school. Rather than do a set of standalone lessons, the artists worked with the classroom teachers on various projects. In one case (as mentioned in Chapter 3), the combined arts/science lesson focused on the essential question "How do we observe?" Students were first asked to draw a picture of leaves from memory. They then went to a local arboretum and observed the parts of a leaf. Then the students were asked to draw again. The before-and-after elements of these drawings showed the progress the students had made in both artistic and scientific knowledge; by completing this project, the artists and teachers showed the overlap in their fields.

The principal showed examples of student observations from across the grade levels, from young students drawing a view (from the same window) of the seasons over the year, to older elementary students drawing the human skeletal system. Where did the principal get these artifacts? He linked to artifacts in the students' portfolios. The principal had his own reflection on the work, but the portfolio was very much centered on the activity and products generated in the classroom by the students and teachers.

The superintendent reviewed the portfolios online and discussed the work with the principals in one-on-one performance reviews. Then, using a rubric that was district-approved (and generated with input from both the principals and the superintendent), the portfolios were scored.

Teachers can also create their own portfolios. The structure for the artifacts is based on Charlotte Danielson's Framework for Teaching (2007). Like the principals, teachers can draw on elements within their students' portfolios as they generate their own. A teacher can describe the progress of a particular student who has made significant improvement. By showing the student's growth over time, the teacher can demonstrate his or her effectiveness in reaching this student.

In a professional portfolio, the badges can represent both required and optional elements. There may be some things that all teachers are expected to demonstrate: everything from curriculum planning to classroom management to interactions with students and families. The additional badges (sometimes called *microcredentials*) can show achievements that the teacher is pursuing. Perhaps the teacher has done more to learn about working with second-language students, dealing with bullying behaviors, or integrating new technologies into the classroom. It's also a chance for teachers to describe skills that may not show up on a résumé, such as taking a leadership role in planning a professional development activity or applying a new classroom strategy.

Schools and districts can begin to define the badges that teachers can earn, similar to students' individual learning plans. This way, teachers have concrete steps to achieving certain goals. Ultimately, this can pave the way toward teachers working on National Board Certification or other formal structures. Whether the teachers are working toward formal certification or are just honing their skills, the power of collecting, selecting, and reflecting on their work can be highly engaging and can provide a new dynamic to the conversation between principal and teacher.

Connecting to Other Initiatives

If your school is working on new initiatives, such as making your curriculum more contemporary, introducing block schedules, or moving toward project-based learning, the database underneath the digital portfolio can help you address a key question: Does this initiative have an effect on student work? The digital portfolio can also help with the flipside of that question: By looking at student work, what do *we* need to work on?

For example, consider the links between curriculum mapping and digital portfolios (Niguidula, 2010). A curriculum map is a useful way for school faculties to examine how teaching takes place. In its most basic form, a curriculum map is a table, with columns for essential questions, content, skills, assessment, and activities. The table is meant to be chronological, corresponding to the school year.

Mapping has gone through many iterations over the years, and technology tools have helped to make this activity much more of a collaborative project within and across school communities. Maps can help determine our aspirations (*consensus maps* can be a group's description of the way it hopes the curriculum will play out through the year) and also document actual progress (*diary maps* are an individual teacher's journal of the content, skills, and assessments that were actually addressed, written down as the year goes along) (Jacobs, 2004).

Curriculum maps and digital portfolio initiatives can support each other. Simply put, a curriculum map is a description of a teacher's work; a digital portfolio is a collection of a student's work. When used together, schools can have a feedback loop, as shown in Figure 6.4.

FIGURE 6.4 | **Curriculum Map/Student Portfolio Feedback Loop**

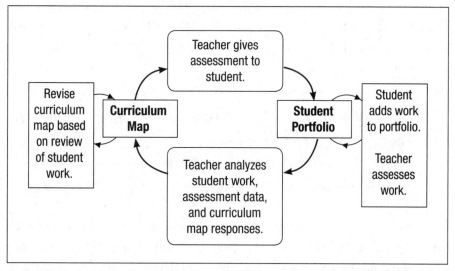

Source: From *Curriculum 21: Essential Education for a Changing World* (p. 161), by Heidi Hayes Jacobs (Ed.), 2010, Alexandria, VA: ASCD.

Let's start on the left side of the loop; at the beginning of the year, the teacher created a curriculum map that outlines the content, skills, and assessments for a course. As the year progresses, we move through the loop: The teacher sets up the assessments, and the students respond in their digital portfolios.

The key point occurs at the bottom of the loop. After the students have submitted some work in their portfolios and the teacher has assessed that work, there can be a moment of teacher reflection. Given the student performances on the assessments, do we need to make adjustments to the curriculum for the year? Perhaps many students need more practice or instruction in some specific content, or perhaps they're doing far better on a skill than the teacher expected. The student work should be a chance for a reality check and to make sure that the teaching practices are adapted to this year's group of students at this particular point of time.

As I've written elsewhere (2010), "the key to the feedback loop is that each step is an *action*" (p. 161). The maps and portfolios contain a great deal of rich data; to make the initiatives truly valuable, that set of data needs to be turned into some action or improve some practice or relationship.

Similarly, the digital portfolio and badge system can help showcase the school as a whole. When one Rhode Island high school was up for accreditation, a faculty committee was charged with showing how classroom activities connect to the school's expectations. The committee met with the whole faculty and went over the list of expectations. Each teacher was asked to select at least one assessment that best demonstrated an expectation. Teachers were to submit

- The instructions for the assignment.
- A notation of which expectation(s) are addressed by the assignment.
- The rubric or other scoring instrument.
- A student response that demonstrated "meeting" the expectation.
- A student response that demonstrated "exceeding" the expectation.

For privacy reasons, student names and any identifying information were removed from the work. (If you plan to show samples of a portfolio to outsiders, you should ask for permission slips from both the student and the teacher that clearly state how you plan to use the artifact and who will review it.)

Because many teacher assignments were already in the digital portfolio system, all the teachers had to do was check off which task (and which student entries) they wanted to submit. The committee then had an electronic list of all the nominated assignments along with the attached student work. With this list, the committee could narrow down which entries would make the most sense to include in the accreditation package.

Procedurally, the digital portfolio did two things. First, it provided *all* of the faculty with an easy way to participate in the process. Because the work was already online (and linked to expectations), the teachers did not have to dig through past years' folders to find appropriate tasks and samples. This helped make the school's submission more reflective of the faculty as a whole (rather than being primarily the work of the accreditation committee). Second, it offered another opportunity to reflect on how the school's expectations are being met. If, for example, the committee found that all of the teacher submissions were linked to the same one or two expectations, questions might arise about the other expectations: Why (for example) did few teachers submit tasks related to the expectation that "all students should know how to learn and achieve collaboratively?" Did the tasks not exist, or did the teachers feel that those tasks didn't represent their best work?

This is how digital portfolios and badges can provide a different type of data-driven change. In this case, the data are not just quantitative; we can see the artifacts the students have developed, as well as the rubrics and other scoring instruments. This information can be just as valuable as the standard numeric breakdowns in showing student, teacher, and school achievements. The ability to sort through such data, especially after the school has been working with portfolios for a while, can be of great help in informing practice.

Putting Students Front and Center

Let's go back to where we started, with Amanda's end-of-year presentation. Through the year, Amanda has worked on her tasks, made progress toward earning her badges, received feedback on her work, and created tours of her accomplishments. There has been a lot of activity online, and now she is ready to talk with the teachers, Ms. C and Mr. G, about her reflection on her work.

In the end, this is perhaps the most important step—the conversation between the teachers and the student, the face-to-face time set aside to talk about the student's goals and achievements, to focus on one student and help that student with what he or she needs.

The best educational technology projects don't start with technology—they start with education. Digital badges can be a powerful tool to show student progress toward a school's goals; collecting the evidence behind those badges into digital portfolios provides a unique insight into each student and to the tasks they have done to reach this point. To truly unleash the power of these tools, the essential question to consider is this: What kinds of conversations do you want to have in your school? Helping students show that they're mastering standards—while allowing them to show who they are as individuals—can transform the way your school serves both your students and your community.

Appendix

Sample Badge Lists

Sample Tour Templates and Rubrics

FIGURE A.1 | **Graduation Badge List, Mt. Hope High School**

Badge	Graduation Portfolio Requirements	Number of Proficient Entries
	1. Listening Effectively (Interactive Listening)	1
	2. Speaking Effectively (Oral Presentations)	1
	3. Report Writing 4. Procedural Writing 5. Persuasive Writing 6. Text-Based Writing	6
	7. Reflective Writing 8. Narrative Writing 9. Poetry Writing	2
	10. Reading and Responding to an Informational Text 11. Reading and Responding to a Literary Text	3
	12. Problem Solving	4
	13. Numbers and Operations 14. Geometry and Measurement 15. Functions and Algebra 16. Data, Statistics, and Probability	6 (must include at least one of each)
	17. Think Sequentially 18. Investigate, Analyze, and Interpret Informational Resources	3
	19. Investigate Through Inquiry 20. Understand Systems and Energy 21. Relate Form to Function 22. Apply Scientific Principles to Real-World Situations	4
	23. Arts	Must earn a Visual Arts, Theater, or Music badge (as determined by those departments)
	24. Technology	Must build a digital portfolio

Source: Mt. Hope High School, Bristol-Warren Regional School District, Rhode Island. Used with permission.

FIGURE A.2 | Graduation Badge List, Tourtellotte Memorial High School

	Expectation 1 **Problem Solving**	The process of effectively applying the analysis, synthesis, and evaluative processes in both independent and group settings to enable productive problem solving
	Expectation 2 **Communication: A.** **Interactive Communication**	The process of understanding, organizing/developing, speaking, listening/responding, and collaborating
	Expectation 2 **Communication:** **B. Reading**	The process of understanding, interpreting, connecting to, and forming a critical stance on textual material
	Expectation 2 **Communication: C. Writing**	The process of expressing ideas through writing in a variety of forms, using standard language conventions and considering various audiences
	Expectation 3 **Information, Media, and** **Technology Skills**	The process of ethically using a variety of 21st century tools to acquire and disseminate information, solve authentic problems, and increase productivity
	Expectation 4 **Innovative Thinking**	The process of demonstrating originality, creativity, flexibility, and adaptability in thinking patterns, work processes, and working/learning conditions
	Expectation 5 **Cultural/Civic** **Awareness and Personal** **Responsibility: A. Cultural** **Awareness**	The process of understanding diverse cultures, recognizing global relationships, and responding independently to changing conditions
	Expectation 5 **Cultural/Civic** **Awareness and Personal** **Responsibility:** **B. Civic Awareness**	The process of understanding social responsibility in relation to community
	Expectation 5 **Cultural/Civic** **Awareness and Personal** **Responsibility: C. Personal** **Responsibility**	The process of understanding personal accountability and its effects on quality of life

Source: Tourtellotte Memorial High School, North Grosvenordale, Connecticut. Used with permission.

FIGURE A.3 | **Graduation Badge List, Putnam High School**

Academic Learning Expectations		
	1. Read actively	For each expectation • Students will include one completed entry (with summary, artifact, and reflection) for each grade level (9, 10, 11, 12). • Each entry must be assessed on a schoolwide rubric and be approved by a teacher.
	2A. Written communication	
	2B. Oral communication	
	3. Individual work	
	4. Group work	
	5. Problem solving	
	6. Using technology	
Civic and Social Expectations		
	7. Demonstrates personal and civic responsibility	Students must • Earn a physical fitness badge and • Earn a badge in "Understanding Responsibilities" or "School Community Involvement."
	8. Makes positive contributions within the school and community	Students must • Complete 20 hours of community service, maintained in a log.
	9. Respects, promotes, and celebrates diversity	Students must • Satisfy the expectation through school community involvement or demonstrate understanding of diversity through academics (one over four years) and • Demonstrate understanding of diversity through the arts (one over four years).

Source: Putnam High School, Putnam, Connecticut. Used with permission.

FIGURE A.4 | **High School Expectations, Narragansett High School**

	NHS1.1 Communicate effectively using oral, written, and technological formats.	5 complete entries from at least 3 subject areas Subject areas are defined as: 1. English 2. Math 3. Science 4. Social studies 5. Technology 6. Visual and performing arts 7. Unified arts/other (physical education, health, family and consumer science; student independent tasks, and tasks not offered through academic courses). 8. World languages
	NHS1.2 Meet proficiency in content and applied learning standards as outlined in the Rhode Island High School Diploma System.	4 complete entries from at least 3 subject areas
	NHS1.3 Read critically and interpret a wide range of materials with varying degrees of complexity.	4 complete entries from at least 3 subject areas
	NHS1.4 Demonstrate the use of reasoning and problem-solving skills and strategies through analysis and synthesis of data and information.	4 complete entries from at least 3 subject areas
	NHS2.1 Demonstrate the behaviors and skills for independence and collaboration.	5 complete entries
	NHS2.2 Participate as a citizen in the local, national, and global community.	
	NHS2.3 Demonstrate an understanding of and respect for diversity.	2 complete entries
	NHS2.4 Set individual goals for continued lifelong learning.	2 complete entries

Source: Narragansett High School, Narragansett, Rhode Island. Used with permission.

FIGURE A.5 | **High School Expectations, Ponaganset High School**

Number	Performance Graduation Expectations (PGEs)
12	W (Writing): The student **writes** effectively for a variety of purposes and audiences. The proficient student W1 Creates narrative writing by organizing and relating a story line/plot/series of events and applying and demonstrating the use of narrative strategies to engage the reader. W2 Creates informational writing (research papers, reports, procedures, or persuasive writing) that effectively organizes ideas/concepts, conveys purpose, and uses elaboration strategies. W3 Creates analytical writing by responding to literary text, informational text, and other media, showing an understanding of ideas in text and making judgments about text. W4 Creates reflective essays that explore and share thoughts, observations, and impressions about their learning. W5 Creates a scientific lab report by identifying a problem, predicting an outcome, collecting data, and analyzing and evaluating results. W6 Creates a writing in Spanish that effectively organizes ideas, information, opinion, or story.
3	RD (Reading): The student **reads** literary text, informational text, and other media for a variety of purposes. The proficient student RD1 Demonstrates initial understanding of literary text and analyzes and interprets literary texts, citing evidence as appropriate. RD2 Demonstrates initial understanding of informational text and uses strategies to analyze, understand, and interpret informational text across content areas.
7	S (Speaking): The student **speaks**, presents, and converses well. The proficient student S1 Makes a presentation to share information. S2 Converses effectively to exchange ideas as well as express and/or defend a point of view. S3 Makes a presentation in Spanish to share information, role play, or converse to express ideas or a point of view.
6	PS (Problem Solving): The student **solves problems** with creative and critical thinking skills. The proficient student PS1 Identifies a problem, gathers and assesses information, generates and refines solutions, and communicates the findings.
5	RF (Reflecting): The student effectively **reflects** on his/her thinking and/or performance. The proficient student RF1 Identifies strengths and areas that require improvement and communicates ways to improve in the future.

(continued)

FIGURE A.5 | **High School Expectations, Ponaganset High School—(*continued*)**

Number	Performance Graduation Expectations (PGEs)
6	M (Mathematics): The student **utilizes mathematics** to solve relevant (*situational*) problems. The proficient student M1 Demonstrates strategic mathematical knowledge, problem solving, and communication using multiple representations (words, mathematic symbols, tables, graphics, etc.) and justifies work in a logical, fluent manner as to its relevance in solving the problem.
1	C (Civics): The student **displays civic and social responsibility** and initiative. The proficient student C1 Makes a contribution to the community. C2 Recognizes that people have certain rights, responsibilities, and differences.
(Project)	PR (Personal Responsibility): The student **demonstrates personal responsibility**. The proficient student PR1 Shows initiative, self-discipline, good decision making, and perseverance in achieving success. PR2 Shows initiative, self-discipline, good decision making, and perseverance in achieving a healthy lifestyle.
	T (Technology): The student **applies technology.** The proficient student T1 Manipulates technology as a tool to gather, analyze, organize, and present information. [*Successfully completing the digital portfolio will satisfy this requirement.*]

Source: Ponaganset High School, Foster-Glocester Regional School District, Rhode Island. Used with permission.

FIGURE A.6 | **High School Expectations, Rhode Island School for the Deaf**

Expectation #1 (Communication)
All RI School for the Deaf students will express their thoughts and ideas clearly through American Sign Language and written English.

Required Demonstrations:
Students will deliver and reflect on 2 oral presentations.

Expectation #2 (Literacy)
All RI School for the Deaf students will read, decode, comprehend, synthesize, analyze, critique, and reflect on numeric and written information gathered from a variety of sources.

Required Demonstrations:
(1) Students will write and reflect on (a) 2 responses to a work of literature; (b) 2 cause/effect expository essays (1 from social studies/1 from science); (c) 2 compare/contrast expository essays (from 2 different disciplines); (d) 1 lab report; (e) 1 "How to" expository essay; (f) 2 persuasive essays; (g) 1 personal narrative; (h) 1 creative narrative; and (i) 2 formal research papers (from 2 different disciplines).

(2) Students will create and maintain an annotated list of at least 20 significant books read over 4 years.

Expectation #3 (Technology)
All RI School for the Deaf students will be capable of and comfortable with manipulating instruments of technology across all disciplines.

Required Demonstrations:
Students will demonstrate the effective use of technology by performing the following: (1) Use a variety of software and hardware devices in the presentation of their digital graduation portfolios, which further reinforces their ability to access, organize, evaluate, interpret, and communicate information; and (2) Use at least 3 of the following types of software applications/processes as problem-solving strategies to demonstrate informed decision making: word processing, e-mailing with attachment, Internet browser navigation, graphic tools, spreadsheet, and PowerPoint as demonstrated in their digital portfolios.

Expectation #4 (Interdisciplinary Learning)
All RI School for the Deaf students will connect ideas between and among all disciplines and subjects inside and outside the classroom.

Required Demonstrations:
Students must complete the following activities: (1) Create an extended interdisciplinary research project between English and Social Studies, incorporating resources from a variety of in-school and out-of-school sources; and (2) Create an extended interdisciplinary research project between Mathematics and Science, incorporating resources from a variety of in-school and out-of-school sources.

Expectation #5 (Critical Thinking)
All RI School for the Deaf students will see and understand the relationships among different types of knowledge and how to use them to solve current and future learning dilemmas.

(continued)

FIGURE A.6 | **High School Expectations, Rhode Island School for the Deaf**
          —*(continued)*

 (continued)	**Required Demonstrations:** Students will complete an extended Math project in each of the following strands/areas: (a) Number and Operations; (b) Geometry and Measurement; (c) Functions and Algebra; and (d) Data, Statistics, and Probability.
	Expectation #6 (Problem Solving) All RI School for the Deaf students will effectively use problem-solving strategies to formulate questions, interpret relevant information, and generate an appropriate solution to a problem.
	Expectation #7 (Performance in the Arts) All RI School for the Deaf students will develop and exhibit an understanding and appreciation of the visual and performing arts. **Required Demonstrations:** (1) Students will create a work of art applying visual arts concepts using a variety of techniques and processes. Students will then write a reflection of the process to submit with their work of art, or (2) Students will apply technical theater knowledge or act during the performance of a play. Students will then write a reflection on their participation in this theatrical experience.
	Expectation #8 (Personal Responsibility) All RI School for the Deaf students will respect themselves, others, and their property and space. All students will take responsibility for their own actions, words, and work.
	Expectation #9 (Social Responsibility) All RI School for the Deaf students will establish goals that are community based as well as personal and follow through with them. Students will find nonviolent solutions to school, community, and other social problems. **Required Demonstrations:** (1) Students will write an essay, design a project, or facilitate a presentation that analyzes problems from a community-based or global perspective and offers solutions or strategies based on analysis of appropriate information and ideas; and (2) Students will complete 40 hours of service to community or school over 4 years, as well as (a) keep an activity log approved by a supervisor, and (b) generate a reflective statement capturing the personal and social impact of the experience.
	Expectation #10 (Deaf Identity) All RI School for the Deaf students will develop and exhibit a positive understanding of their deaf identity and deaf culture.
	Senior Project All students will complete a senior project consisting of fieldwork, a research paper, and a presentation on a topic of the student's choice.

Source: Rhode Island School for the Deaf, Providence, Rhode Island. Used with permission.

FIGURE A.7 | **Badge Tour (for All Grade Levels)**

Section Title	Description
1. Evidence for the Badge	• You may include evidence from classroom assignments; logs (such as reading logs or community service hours); projects; data points (such as attendance); extracurricular activities; or whatever evidence is needed to complete the badge.
2. Reflection	• How does your evidence demonstrate the badge requirements? Specify the parts of your evidence (such as a passage in an essay or a moment in a video or podcast) that relate to the requirements. • How does this *body* of evidence show your growth as a learner? What strengths does a reader see throughout this collection? Include multiple examples.

FIGURE A.8 | **Best Work Tour (for All Grade Levels)**

In this tour, students select their best work from the year and reflect on it. These tours often have three sections:

Section Title	Description
1. Cover	• Include a picture or video welcoming the reader to your portfolio.
2. Best Work	• Sample prompt: Please select your four best pieces of work from this year. Each entry must have received a score of "3" or better on the schoolwide rubric. Your pieces should all come from different classes.
3. Reflection	• Sample prompt: Please describe why you think each of these pieces represents your best work.

FIGURE A.9 | **Action Plan Tour, 11th Grade, Mt. Hope High School**

Section Title	Description
Personal Statement	Please write a letter of introduction to the reviewer specifically addressing the following prompts: • Name • Grade • Academic accomplishments • What are my interests? • What are my personal/career goals?
Completeness	Contains a report listing all the entries that the student has completed this year and summarizes the progress toward the school's required goals.
Action Plan	Review your Completeness page and identify the proficiency-based graduation requirement (PBGR) categories you have yet to meet. In a well-written narrative, develop an action plan for your senior year by addressing the following prompts: • Identify the categories you will have the opportunity to complete during the remainder of the school year and the tasks you will use to show proficiency. • Think about and identify the courses you will take next year to help you meet the requirements. • What will you need to do in those classes to meet missing PBGRs? (Please do not simply state that you will complete the tasks. Reflect on what you need to do to improve on your skills.)
Best Work	a) Your 11th grade tour should include your best work toward achieving proficiency in your courses. You need to do the following: • Choose 1 completed Communication (PBGR 1-11) project that highlights your skill in that area. • Next, choose an artifact from Problem Solving/Critical Thinking (PBGR 12-23) that highlights your skills in that area. b) Reflect on your strengths in a well-developed, insightful response. In your response, address the following topics in a well-structured, essay format. **Communication**: • What is/are the most important skills or strategies that helped you become a successful communicator? • How does the piece you've included in this section highlight your strengths in this area? • How will these skills help you in the future?

(continued)

FIGURE A.9 | **Action Plan Tour, 11th Grade, Mt. Hope High School—(*continued*)**

Section Title	Description
Best Work—(*continued*)	**Problem Solving/Critical Thinking**: • What are the skills or strategies you use to be successful in problem solving/critical thinking? • How does the piece you've included in this section highlight your strengths in this area? • How will these skills help you in the future?
Work Related to My Interests and Goals	a. Choose one project that is connected to your interests and/or goals for the future. A teacher evaluation is not necessary for this project. b. Reflect on your goals and interests in a well-developed, insightful response. In your response, address the following topics using a well-structured, paragraph format: • Identify your interests and goals after high school. Are they similar? Explain. • Describe the artifact you have chosen to represent your personal interests/goals. • How does the artifact relate to your interest/future goals? • What courses are you taking this year and/or next year that relate to this interest/goal? What are other ways in which you plan to pursue this interest/goal?

Source: Mt. Hope High School, Bristol-Warren Regional School District, Rhode Island. Used with permission.

FIGURE A.10 | **Action Plan Tour Rubric, 11th Grade, Mt. Hope High School**

11TH GRADE ACTION PLAN RUBRIC

	Advanced (4)	Proficient (3)	Developing (2)	Emerging (1)
Part I: Personal Statement Weight: 5	Personal statement is compelling and inspirational and allows the evaluator to learn much about the student. ☐	Personal statement includes all required elements: name, grade, personal and academic accomplishments and allows the evaluator to learn about the student. ☐	Personal statement is missing some of the required elements; connection to the student is incomplete. ☐	Fails to write a personal statement. ☐
Part II: Proficiency-Based Graduation Requirements (PBGRs) Summary Weight: 15		Student has met proficiency in all of the required categories. ☐	Student has met proficiency in all but two of the required categories. ☐	Student has not met proficiency in three or more categories. ☐
Part III: Action Plan Weight: 5	Student identifies categories/requirements needed and provides a detailed description of his/her action plan for senior year. ☐	Student identifies PBGRs not met and explains why these have not been met. Student explains plan to meet missing PBGRs including strategies, courses, and how to improve skills. ☐	Student identifies some categories/requirements needed and provides a general description of the action plan for senior year. ☐	Student's requirements are not linked with the action plan for senior year. ☐

(continued)

FIGURE A.10 | **Action Plan Tour Rubric, 11th Grade, Mt. Hope High School**—*(continued)*

11TH GRADE ACTION PLAN RUBRIC

	Advanced (4)	Proficient (3)	Developing (2)	Emerging (1)
Part IV: Strengths Weight: 5	Student describes detailed connections between artifacts and the skill area. Student presents a well-crafted, developed, and convincing argument that he/she has met proficiency in each of the categories (communication and problem solving).	Student effectively describes connections between artifact and communication *and* problem-solving/critical thinking skills. Student presents a developed, convincing argument that he/she has met proficiency in communication *and* problem-solving/critical thinking skills.	Student's description of connections between artifacts and the identified skill area is only acceptable for some artifacts. Student presents a poorly developed, unconvincing argument that he/she has met proficiency in each of the categories (communication and problem solving).	Student's description of connections between artifact and the identified skill area is not acceptable for either artifact. Student's argument that he/she has met proficiency is not discernible or is absent.
	☐	☐	☐	☐
Part V: Interests and Goals Weight: 5	Student identifies area of interest/goals. Student makes detailed connection between artifacts and interests and goals. Student provides a detailed explanation of how he/she will pursue their interests over the next school year.	Student identifies area of interest/goals. Student makes connection between artifacts and interests and goals. Student explains how he/she will pursue their interests and goals over the next school year.	Student identifies area of interest/goals. Student attempts to make a connection between artifacts and interests and goals, but relationship is sometimes unclear. Student does not fully explain how he/she will pursue their interests over the next school year.	Student fails to identify the area of interest/goals *or* fails to identify the specific plan toward pursuing this area of interest or meeting these goals. Connection between artifacts and interests and goals is inadequate or not done. Student does not provide an explanation of how he/she will pursue their interests over the next school year.
	☐	☐	☐	☐

Presentation Weight: 5			
Student skillfully engages audience by demonstrating poise and confidence.	Student effectively engages audience by demonstrating poise and confidence.	Student ineffectively engages audience; attempts to demonstrate poise and confidence.	Student attempts but fails to engage audience and fails to demonstrate poise and confidence.
Student skillfully adapts to audience, maintaining interest.	Student effectively adapts to audience, maintaining interest.	Student ineffectively adapts to audience.	Student attempts but fails to adapt to audience and fails to maintain interest.
Student skillfully uses language appropriate to audience, context, and purpose.	Student effectively uses language appropriate to audience, context, and purpose.	Student ineffectively uses language appropriate to audience, context, and purpose.	Student attempts but fails to use language appropriate to audience, context, and purpose.
Student skillfully uses appropriate eye contact.	Student effectively uses appropriate eye contact.	Student communicates ineffectively; has difficulty using appropriate eye contact.	Student attempts but fails to use appropriate eye contact.
Student skillfully maintains a volume and pace that enhance communication.	Student effectively maintains volume and pace that enhance communication.	Student inconsistently maintains volume and pace that enhance communication.	Student attempts but fails to maintain volume and pace that enhance communication.
Student skillfully uses appropriate pronunciation and enunciation.	Student effectively uses appropriate pronunciation and enunciation.	Student inconsistently uses appropriate pronunciation and enunciation.	Student attempts but fails to use appropriate pronunciation and enunciation.
Student skillfully uses posture, demeanor, and gestures appropriate to task.	Student effectively uses posture, demeanor, and gestures appropriate to task.	Student ineffectively uses posture, demeanor, and gestures appropriate to task.	Student attempts but fails to use posture, demeanor, and gestures appropriate to task.
☐	☐	☐	☐

(continued)

FIGURE A.10 | Action Plan Tour Rubric, 11th Grade, Mt. Hope High School—*(continued)*

11TH GRADE ACTION PLAN RUBRIC

	Advanced (4)	Proficient (3)	Developing (2)	Emerging (1)
Level of Professionalism Relative to Dress, Appearance, and Demeanor Weight: 2		Student is neat, has appropriate dress, is courteous, is punctual, and is prepared for the presentation. ☐	Student has attempted to dress appropriately and has prepared somewhat for the presentation. ☐	Student dresses inappropriately; has arrived late and/or is not prepared for the presentation. ☐
Evaluator Comments				

Source: Mt. Hope High School, Bristol-Warren Regional School District, Rhode Island. Used with permission.

FIGURE A.11 | **Growth over Time Tour, Mt. Hope High School**

Section Title	Description	Details
Cover	The cover of the portfolio is your introduction to your panel of judges. Include a picture of yourself or something that you are passionate about. Also include an introduction of yourself. Your introduction should summarize what you want someone to know about you, provide some insight into your high school journey, and preview what will be contained in the rest of the portfolio. *Think of this as the introductory paragraph in an essay.* **Presentation Notes:** When you give your presentation, you do not need to read the statement you wrote. Simply summarize it for the panel.	Student can add photo/image/video. Student includes a written introduction/personal statement.
Proficiency-Based Graduation Requirement (PBGR) Summary	For your senior presentation, all categories must be checked for the portfolio to be complete.	Overview of artifacts in portfolio
Growth over Time	In this section, you will describe the area in which you have shown the most growth during your high school career. This can be general content (science, math, English); a skill (oral presentation); or a general skill (time management). You must have evidence (graded tasks) to support whatever you are saying is your growth area. This means including the details on how the two or more pieces show your growth and the steps you took to improve in that area.	Student must include two artifacts but has the option to include more. Student includes a summary detailing the growth over time and describes the events/process that led to this growth.

(continued)

FIGURE A.11 | **Growth over Time Tour, Mt. Hope High School—(*continued*)**

Section Title	Description	Details
My Strengths	In this section, you will describe the area that has been your greatest strength during the course of high school. This can be general content (English, music, social studies); a skill (writing); or a general skill (maturity). You must have evidence (graded tasks) to support whatever you are saying is your strength area. This means including the details on how the two or more pieces show your strength in that area.	Student must include two artifacts but has the option to include more. Student includes a summary identifying an area of strength and details how the submissions demonstrate that this is an area of strength.
Area of Interest	In this section you will discuss your area(s) of interest. You need to have at least one assignment from a class, but you may also include supplemental activities that you are involved in or have completed that demonstrate your interests.	Student must include one artifact but has the option to include more.
Future Planning	In this section you will discuss your future plans or next steps. You do not necessarily have to have definitive plans, but you should show that you have thought about what the next stage of your life will include. You may choose to upload examples that demonstrate your future planning (college acceptances, military career).	Student may upload artifacts but it is not mandatory.

Source: Mt. Hope High School, Bristol-Warren Regional School District, Rhode Island. Used with permission.

FIGURE A.12 | Growth over Time Tour Rubric, Mt. Hope High School

	Advanced	Proficient	Developing	Emerging
Proficiency-Based Graduation Requirements (PBGRs) Summary	Student has exceeded minimum proficiency in several of the required categories. ☐	Student has met proficiency in all of the required categories. ☐	Student has not met proficiency in one or two of the required categories. ☐	Student has not met proficiency in three or more categories. ☐
Growth over Time	Student details exceptional growth as a learner, specifying a skill area and supplying excellent, detailed examples. Student uses the two artifacts to show and describe the area/skill in which he/she has shown growth, with specific examples provided. Student details the strategies and timeline that led to improvement in the skill area. ☐	Student reflects on growth as a learner, specifying a skill area and providing examples. Student is able to use the two artifacts to show and describe the area/skill in which he/she has shown growth. Student describes the strategies that led to improvement in the skill area. ☐	Student provides a general reflection on growth as a learner or specifies a skill area but does not provide examples Student describes the area/skill that he/she has shown growth in, but has difficulty using the artifacts to support his/her statements. Student gives a vague description of the strategies that led to improvement in the skill area. ☐	Student attempts to use the two selected artifacts as evidence, but the artifacts show little or no growth in the ability to apply skills. Student's choice of artifacts does not demonstrate the indicated growth area. Student is unable to provide examples of strategies that were used to improve the skill area. ☐

(continued)

FIGURE A.12 | **Growth over Time Tour Rubric, Mt. Hope High School**—*(continued)*

	Advanced	Proficient	Developing	Emerging
My Strengths	Student presents a developed, convincing argument that the skill area stated is a strength. Student describes detailed connections between the artifacts and the skill area. More than two proficient artifacts or two advanced artifacts are presented in the stated skill area. ☐	Student presents a developed argument that the skill area stated is a strength. Student describes connections between the artifacts and the identified skill area. Two proficient artifacts are presented in the skill area. ☐	Student presents a poorly developed argument that he/she has met proficiency in this category. Student has difficulty describing connections between the artifacts and the identified skill area. Two artifacts are presented in the skill area. ☐	Student presents a poorly developed, unconvincing argument that he/she has met proficiency in this category. Student is unable to describe connections between the artifacts and the identified skill area. Student does not provide two artifacts in the presented skill area. ☐
Area of Interest	Student identifies the area of interest and connects to future planning. Student provides more than one artifact that clearly demonstrates the area of interest. ☐	Student identifies the area of interest. Student provides one artifact that demonstrates the area of interest. ☐	Student identifies the area of interest. Student provides an artifact that has a casual link to the area of interest. ☐	Student fails to identify the area of interest. *or* Student does not provide an artifact to demonstrate the area of interest. ☐

	☐	☐	☐	☐
Future Planning	There is ample evidence of future planning. Student has a post-graduation plan that may include acceptance to a college, certification program, military, or job. Student is able to make detailed connections about how their learning and growth during the course of high school have helped them plan for the future.	There is adequate evidence of future planning. Student has a post-graduation plan, has completed steps of the plan, but has yet to finalize a decision. Student is able to make connections about how their learning and growth during the course of high school have helped them plan for the future.	There is some evidence of future planning. Student has ideas but has not yet decided on a definitive path for after graduation. Student has difficulty making connections about how their learning and growth during the course of high school have helped them plan for the future.	Student is unable to articulate their plan for the future. Student has little to no ideas on a post-graduation plan. Student is unable to make connections about how their learning and growth during the course of high school have helped them plan for the future.
Presentation	Student skillfully engages audience by demonstrating poise and confidence. Student skillfully adapts to audience, maintaining interest. Student skillfully uses language appropriate to audience, context, and purpose. Student skillfully uses appropriate eye contact.	Student effectively engages audience by demonstrating poise and confidence. Student effectively adapts to audience, maintaining interest. Student effectively uses language appropriate to audience, context, and purpose. Student effectively uses appropriate eye contact.	Student ineffectively engages audience; attempts to demonstrate poise and confidence. Student ineffectively adapts to audience. Student ineffectively uses language appropriate to audience, context, and purpose. Student communicates ineffectively; has difficulty using appropriate eye contact.	Student attempts but fails to engage audience and fails to demonstrate poise and confidence. Student attempts but fails to adapt to audience and fails to maintain interest. Student attempts but fails to use language appropriate to audience, context, and purpose. Student attempts but fails to use appropriate eye contact.

(continued)

FIGURE A.12 | **Growth over Time Tour Rubric, Mt. Hope High School—(*continued*)**

	Advanced	Proficient	Developing	Emerging
Presentation— (*continued*)	Student skillfully maintains volume and pace that enhance communication. Student skillfully uses appropriate pronunciation and enunciation. ☐	Student maintains volume and pace that enhance communication. Student effectively uses appropriate pronunciation and enunciation. ☐	Student inconsistently maintains volume and pace that enhance communication. Student consistently uses appropriate pronunciation and enunciation. ☐	Student attempts but fails to maintain volume and pace that enhance communication. Student attempts but fails to use appropriate pronunciation and enunciation. ☐
Level of Professionalism Relative to Dress, Appearance, and Demeanor	Student is dressed professionally, maintains appropriate demeanor throughout, is punctual, and is clearly prepared for the presentation. ☐	Student is neat, has appropriate dress, is courteous, is punctual, and is prepared for the presentation. ☐	Student has attempted to dress appropriately and has prepared somewhat for the presentation. ☐	Student dresses inappropriately, has arrived late, or is not prepared for the presentation. ☐
	Advanced	Proficient		Unacceptable
Overall Presentation	Student's presentation went above and beyond the requirements of a successful graduation presentation. ☐	Student's presentation met all the requirements of a successful graduation presentation. ☐		Student's presentation did not meet the minimum requirements for a successful graduation presentation. Student will need to present again to meet graduation requirement. ☐

Source: Mt. Hope High School, Bristol-Warren Regional School District, Rhode Island. Used with permission.

FIGURE A.13 | **End-of-Year Tour, 9th Grade, Ponaganset High School**

Sections	Requirements
Cover **1. Are You on Track?**	Are you on track to graduate? You should currently have at least 8 acceptable entries in your portfolio, with 1 entry from each of your courses. • If you are not on track, explain why you are not and what actions you will take to get back on track and have at least 17 acceptable entries by the end of next year. Please remember that students who are not on track as of the fall lose the privilege of participating in athletics, clubs, and social events.
2. Growth as a Learner	Choose one entry that has helped you grow as a learner this year. It doesn't have to be your best work, but it should be work that challenged you and improved certain knowledge and/or skills. • Provide name of entry. • Describe in detail why you feel this entry helped you grow as a learner. • Clearly identify the skill(s) and/or the knowledge you have gained through the completion of the entry. • Explain the challenge that the entry provided and how you met the challenge.
3. Ponaganset Graduation Expectation (PGE) Strength and Need/ Academic Goal Setting	To graduate from Ponaganset High School (PHS), you must demonstrate that you've met a variety of PGEs. • Choose one PGE that is an area of strength for you and explain why. Choose one entry from your portfolio that clearly demonstrates that a related PGE is an area of strength for you. • Choose one PGE that is an area in need of improvement. Explain why and what you should do to improve in this area. Please refer to the Academic Goals section of the ILP and feel free to use some of what you've already written. • Identify one academic goal for the upcoming school year. Explain why you chose this goal and what you plan to do to improve in this area. Please refer to the Academic Goals section of the ILP and feel free to use some of what you've already written. Also, consult the ILP Sample Goals sheet.
4. Life After High School/Career Goal Setting	You have already begun to explore possible careers and set career goals in your ILP. From your Career Cluster Survey: • Which career cluster(s) is identified? Which of these career(s) interests you? • Which career(s) interested you the most?

(continued)

FIGURE A.13 | **End-of-Year Tour, 9th Grade, Ponaganset High School—(*continued*)**

Sections	Requirements
4. Life After High School/Career Goal Setting—(*continued*)	• Clearly state your current career goal(s). Explain. Please refer to the Postsecondary Goals section of the ILP and feel free to use some of what you've already written. • Did you take any courses this year that align to your career goals? If so, name them and explain how they are aligned. • Are you planning on taking any courses next year that align to your potential career goals? Please explain which courses and how they may be aligned to your career goals. • What resources may you need to reach this goal?
5. Résumé	Upload a copy of your current résumé here. After building your résumé, what can you do to improve on your achievements and accomplishments to meet your goals?
6. Advice to a New 9th Grader	If you could give one piece of advice to an 8th grader who will be heading to PHS in the fall, what would it be and why?

Source: Ponaganset High School, Foster-Glocester Regional School District, Rhode Island. Used with permission.

FIGURE A.14 | **End-of-Year Tour Rubric, 9th Grade, Ponaganset High School**

"Weight" indicates the multiplier for that row. For example, if a student scores an "Advanced" (4) on the first row, which has a weight of 8, the student receives 32 total points for this row of the rubric. In this rubric, the maximum number of points is 100.

"Prorated" means that the student has not been in attendance for the full year at this school.

	4	3	2	1	0	SCORE
1a. On Track to Graduate Weight: *8*	Portfolio is on track with 8 acceptable entries *or* 1 entry for 100% of classes taken (if prorated)	Portfolio is not on track with 7 acceptable entries *or* 1 entry for approx. 85% of classes taken (if prorated)	Portfolio is not on track with 6 acceptable entries *or* 1 entry for approx. 75% of classes taken (if prorated)	Portfolio is not on track with 4–5 acceptable entries *or* 1 entry for approx. 50–65% of classes taken (if prorated)	0–3 entries *or* entries for < 50% of classes	
1b. Steps for Improvement (only for students who are not on track) Weight: *0*	Identifies areas for improvement and provides detailed steps for improving work in the future	Identifies areas for improvement and provides steps for the future	Identifies areas of improvement, but steps for improvement are incomplete or do not make sense	No clear delineation of steps for improvement	No attempt	
2. Growth as a Learner Weight: *3*	In-depth and insightful reflection that includes -clear identification of learned skills and knowledge	Good reflection on the work that includes -identification of learned skills and knowledge	Basic reflection on the work, where there is a genuine attempt to -identify learned skills and knowledge	Reflection is largely incomplete; a poor attempt.	No attempt	

(continued)

FIGURE A.14 | **End-of-Year Tour Rubric, 9th Grade, Ponaganset High School—(continued)**

	4	3	2	1	0	SCORE
2. Growth as a Learner Weight: 3—(continued)	-substantive discussion of the challenge the entry provided includes supporting examples	- discussion of the challenge the entry provided	-discuss the challenge the entry provides However, some of the reflection is unclear or incomplete			
3. Ponaganset Graduation Expectation (PGE) Strength and Need Weight: 5	Student clearly identifies one PGE that is an area of strength and one PGE that is an area of weakness. Creates an in-depth and insightful reflection that discusses why these PGEs were chosen and how the student will respond to the identified area of weakness Identifies and explains current academic goal with in-depth plan to meet goal	Student clearly identifies one PGE that is an area of strength and one PGE that is an area of weakness. Creates an in-depth reflection that discusses why these PGEs were chosen and how the student will respond to the identified area of weakness Identifies and explains current academic goal with plan to meet goal	Student clearly identifies one PGE that is an area of strength and one PGE that is an area of weakness. Creates an adequate reflection that discusses why these PGEs were chosen and how the student will respond to the identified area of weakness	Student fails to clearly identify one PGE that is an area of strength and one that is an area of weakness. Fails to effectively reflect on why these PGEs were chosen Failure to identify current academic goal *and/or* No evidence of plans to improve PGE weakness and meet academic goals		

3. Ponaganset Graduation Expectation (PGE) Strength and Need Weight: 5—(continued)		Identifies and explains current academic goal with little evidence of a plan to meet goal		
		or		
		Student clearly identifies only one PGE that is an area of strength or weakness.		
		Creates an in-depth reflection that discusses why this PGE was chosen and how the student will respond to the identified area of weakness.		
		Identifies and explains current academic goal with little evidence of a plan to meet goal.		

(continued)

FIGURE A.14 | **End-of-Year Tour Rubric, 9th Grade, Ponaganset High School**—*(continued)*

	4	3	2	1	0	SCORE
4. Life After High School Weight: 4	Student effectively responds to all aspects of the prompt and supports responses with details and/or examples.	Student effectively responds to the following aspects of the prompt: - identification of top work values from Career Cluster Survey - identification of careers of most interest and career goal - identification of current/future courses aligned to career goal -identification of resources that may be used to meet goal	Student effectively responds to three aspects of the prompt.	Student effectively responds to one or two aspects of the prompt. The overall response is largely incomplete.	No attempt	
5. Résumé Weight: 1	Student's résumé is uploaded. -student effectively states and explains plans for improving résumé	Student's résumé is uploaded. -student effectively states plans for improving résumé	Student's résumé is uploaded. -student makes a poor attempt to state ways to improve résumé	Student's résumé is uploaded. -student makes no attempt to state ways to improve résumé	No attempt	

				No attempt
6. Advice to a New 9th Grader Weight: 1	In-depth and insightful reflection on success or failure this year. Includes -explicit and clear identification of one piece of advice -well-developed explanation of how the advice will improve the new 9th grader's success	Good reflection on success or failure this year and includes - identification of one piece of advice - explanation of how the advice will improve the new 9th grader's success	Basic reflection on success or failure this year. Inconsistent but genuine attempt to -identify one piece of advice -explain how the advice will improve the new 9th grader's success	Reflection is largely incomplete; a poor attempt
Oral Communication Weight: 2	Delivery (including eye contact, speaking voice, posture, and gestures) is natural, comfortable, and appropriate. Quality of delivery adds to presentation's effectiveness.	Delivery is natural, comfortable, and appropriate. Delivery is consistent.	Delivery is inconsistent, and elements may be distracting at times.	Delivery is highly distracting or disruptive, decreasing effectiveness of presentation.	No attempt

(continued)

FIGURE A.14 | **End-of-Year Tour Rubric, 9th Grade, Ponaganset High School—(continued)**

	4	3	2	1	0	SCORE
RF (Reflecting on Performance) Weight: 1	Includes well-chosen and specific facts and details relevant to the controlling idea to create depth of reflection Applies sophisticated organizational structures within paragraphs / oral comments that enhance the progression of ideas Uses precise and descriptive language which clarifies and supports the reflection Skillfully applies the rules and mechanics of writing / speaking: making no errors	Includes sufficient facts and details to effectively support the main points of the reflection Applies organizational structures within paragraphs / oral comments that support a progression of ideas Uses language which clarifies and supports intent by questioning, comparing, connecting, interpreting, or analyzing Consistently applies the rules and mechanics of writing/speaking (e.g., punctuation, spelling, word usage) making unobtrusive errors	Includes facts and details relevant to the purpose or the main focus Applies some organizational structures within paragraphs / oral comments that allows for a progression of ideas Uses language which partially supports intent Applies the rules and mechanics of writing: making occasional obtrusive errors	Includes irrelevant facts to the purpose or main idea Applies few organizational structures that allows for a progression of ideas Uses language which does not support intent Inconsistently applies the rules and mechanics of writing / speaking: making repetitive errors	No attempt	
					TOTAL SCORE:	

Source: Ponaganset High School, Foster-Glocester Regional School District, Rhode Island. Used with permission.

FIGURE A.15 | **End-of-Year Tour, 10th Grade, Ponaganset High School**

Sections	Requirements
1. Are You on Track?	Are you on track to graduate, based on the fact that you should currently have at least 17 acceptable entries in your portfolio? Were each of the new entries added this year from a different course? • If not, explain why you are not on track and what actions you will be taking to get yourself back on track and have at least 26 acceptable entries by the end of next year. Please remember that students who are not on track lose the privilege of participating in athletics, clubs, and social events.
2. Growth as a Learner	Choose at least two pieces of work in your portfolio that demonstrate growth over time in a particular skill area or PGE. Compare and contrast these two pieces of work, providing specific examples that demonstrate this growth. • Describe in detail why you feel this entry helped you grow as a learner. You should clearly identify the skill(s) and/or the knowledge you have gained through the completion of the entry.
3. Ponaganset Graduation Requirement (PGE) Need/Academic Goal Setting	To graduate from Ponaganset High School (PHS), you must demonstrate that you've met a variety of PGEs. Last year we asked you to look at the PGEs and to identify and explain which one is a strength and which one is an area in need of improvement. • Review what PGE (or learner outcome) you identified as an area in need of improvement last year. How did you propose to respond to this need for improvement? • Now that it is a year later, reflect on your progress. Did you improve upon it? If so, how? If not, why not? • Now answer the same question again for this year: Choose one PGE that is an area in need of improvement for you. Explain why and what you should do in the next year to improve in this PGE. You may choose the same PGE as a continuing weakness, but you must develop a new plan to address this need. • Please identify one academic goal for the upcoming school year. Explain why you chose this goal and what you plan to do to improve in this area. Use the goals in your ILP goals or the Sample ILP Goals sheet for assistance. Please refer to the Academic Goals section of the ILP and feel free to use some of what you've already written.
4. Life After High School/Career Goal Setting	What are your career goals for life beyond high school? • Go back to last year's tour. What goals for life after high school did you state then? • From your Career Cluster Survey: Which career cluster(s) is identified? Which of these career(s) interests you? • Clearly state your current career goal.

(continued)

FIGURE A.15 | **End-of-Year Tour, 10th Grade, Ponaganset High School—(*continued*)**

Sections	Requirements
4. Life After High School/Career Goal Setting—(*continued*)	• What resources may you need to reach this goal? For example, setting up an appointment with your counselor, job shadowing, additional tutorial, career planning, etc. Please refer to the Postsecondary Goals section of the ILP and feel free to use some of what you've already written. You can also refer to the career roadmap section of your ILP for a list of resources you may have already used or plan to use in the future. • What is your academic plan in high school and beyond to meet these goals? List the courses you will take next year to help you achieve your academic goal. Explain how these courses will help you meet your academic goal.
5. Résumé	Upload a copy of your current résumé here. Feel free to update last year's résumé. If you have completed the Employment/Internship/Volunteer Experience Activities section of the ILP, you can use it to help build your résumé. Does your current résumé reflect that you are working toward your career goal? How so? After building your résumé, what can you do to improve on your achievements and accomplishments to meet your goals?

Source: Ponaganset High School, Foster-Glocester Regional School District, Rhode Island. Used with permission.

FIGURE A.16 | **End-of-Year Tour, 11th Grade, Ponaganset High School**

Sections	Requirements
1. Are You on Track?	Are you currently on track to graduate? Your portfolio should now be nearly complete, with at least 26 acceptable entries and 6 of the 7 PGEs met. In addition, were the new entries added this year each from a different course? • If any of these requirements are not met, explain why you are not on track and what actions you will be taking to get yourself back on track. Please remember that students who are not on track lose the privilege of participating in athletics, clubs, and social events. • If you have met these requirements, *congratulations!* You have completed your Ponaganset High School graduation portfolio! Next year, all you will be required to enter into the portfolio is your senior research paper and senior exhibition.
2. Growth as a Learner	How does the portfolio provide evidence that you have grown as a learner over time? • First, define one area of knowledge or one skill (one PGE or learner outcome). • Next, select at least 2 artifacts from your portfolio (including 1 from this school year) that focus on one area of knowledge or skill that you have improved upon while at Ponaganset. • Clearly state which PGE you have selected. • Reflect on how you have grown as a learner over time. Use specific examples from these sources of evidence to demonstrate the specific types of improvements that you have made.
3. My Best Ponaganset Graduation Expectation (PGE)	Which PGE is best supported by the overall body of work in your portfolio? This is not necessarily the number of entries, but the quality of the entries. • Select one PGE to discuss. • Select at least 2 entries with different learner outcomes to provide evidence that you are proficient in this PGE. Make sure to include work from this current year. • Clearly state which PGE you have selected. Reflect on how the evidence you selected proves that you are proficient in this PGE. Be certain to talk about what each specific entry proves about what you know and are able to do.
4. Life After High School/Career Goal Setting	You are approximately 1 year away from graduating high school. What are your academic and career goals beyond high school, and how will you meet these goals? Answer all of the following: • Go back to last year's tour. What career goals did you state then? • Go to the career inventory site to explore your career choices. • What were your top work values? • Which career(s) interested you the most? • Clearly state your current career goal.

(continued)

FIGURE A.16 | **End-of-Year Tour, 11th Grade, Ponaganset High School—(*continued*)**

Sections	Requirements
4. Life After High School/Career Goal Setting—(*continued*)	• How will you further explore your future career choices? For example, job shadow, research job outlook, research education requirements, or job-training programs, etc. • What is your academic plan in high school and beyond to meet these goals? • List the courses you will take next year to help you achieve your academic goal. Explain how these courses will help you meet that goal.
5. Résumé	Upload a copy of your current résumé here. Feel free to update last year's résumé. See the "Info" section for a résumé template and sample résumé. Does your current résumé reflect that you are working toward your career goal? How so? After building your résumé, what can you do to improve on your achievements and accomplishments to meet your goals?
6. Senior Research Paper and Exhibition	What is your proposed topic of interest for your senior research paper and exhibition? • Create a link to your junior English research paper here. Connect the skills you've learned in writing your junior English paper to the skills you'll need to complete your senior research paper. • Type in your topic proposal for your senior research paper. • Type in a brief summary of your proposed senior exhibition learning stretch. • Explain why you chose this topic of interest. Is this topic a passion of yours? If not, are you prepared to spend the next year focusing on a topic that is not? Explain.
7. Community Service	Create a link to your community service project. • Explain the community service you completed. • If you have not completed your community service project, please explain the project you plan to complete next year.

Source: Ponaganset High School, Foster-Glocester Regional School District, Rhode Island

FIGURE A.17 | **Senior Project Portfolio Tour Requirements, Narragansett High School**

As part of its graduation requirements, Narragansett High School students complete a Senior Project in the 12th grade. As they begin the project, students are told:

"You will be challenged to delve into an area of curiosity or passion, to explore a core question or issue in depth, and to demonstrate the acquired knowledge and expertise through a formal oral presentation."

The formal oral presentation is when students present their project to a panel, which includes faculty and administrators as well as members of the community. To prepare for the presentation, students create a tour as follows:

The senior project portfolio tour documents your journey through the senior project. Your portfolio gives the senior project presentation judges an opportunity to become acquainted with you and your project before your presentation. This is their first impression of you, so make it a good one. Through viewing your portfolio, the judges should (will) experience your personal style (personality), as well as view the record of your project.

Your portfolio tour must include the following items in the order listed:

1. Title	Include your full name and/or "senior project portfolio"

2. Sign of Commitment	After your senior project proposal and research paper proposal are approved, you will create a sign of commitment, which will be displayed in school and on the senior project website. This sign announces to the school community your project topic, research paper focus, fieldwork, and final product.
	
	 Although creativity is encouraged, you must follow these guidelines:
	
	 1. Your sign must be 8 ½" X 11" in size.
	 2. Your sign must include:
	   a. your name.
	   b. your project topic, research paper focus, fieldwork, and final product.
	   c. a symbol or graphic to represent the project and fieldwork to be performed.
	   d. a photo of you (no larger than 2" x 2"). It can be your senior photo, a favorite photo of yourself, or your image superimposed onto a graphic or symbol on your sign.
	 3. Typed text is required.

3. Letter of Introduction to the Judges	Your letter of introduction to the judges is your opportunity to tell the judges who you are and why you chose your area of study. It should include your thoughts, selection process, learning stretch, and a thank you to the judges. This gives the judges a glimpse of you and your project before your presentation begins.
4. Time/Cost Analysis	Your time/cost analysis was part of the senior project proposal process. You identified the resources necessary to complete your senior project with success, on time, and within an approved budget.

(continued)

FIGURE A.17 | **Senior Project Portfolio Tour Requirements, Narragansett High School —(continued)**

5. Mentor Agreement Letter	Your mentor agreement letter must be a scanned copy of the document signed by you and your mentor.
6. Senior Project Proposal	Your senior project proposal must be the final version (which includes any modifications) approved by the senior project review board. You must upload a scanned copy of your proposal with your signature.
7. Proposal Approval Sheet	The proposal approval sheet must be a scanned copy of the approval signed by the senior project review board.
8. Planning Process Reflection	This reflection is your chance to look back on the initial stages of your senior project experience, from the moment you decided on a senior project topic through the time when your project was approved by the senior project review board.
9. Final version of your Research Paper, including works cited page	This is a clean copy of your proficient research paper. If your research paper was not graded "proficient" by your English teacher, you may use the version scored "proficient" by the extended school day instructor.
10. Research Paper Reflection	This reflection is your opportunity to look back on the entire process of completing your research paper, from selecting your topic, to conducting your research, to writing and revising the paper.
11. Thank You Letter to Your Mentor	
12. Mentoring Time Log	Your mentoring time log provides documentation of your fieldwork. Your mentor will acknowledge the time spent and summarize the work done for your senior project at each mentoring session. You must use a scanned copy of the completed mentoring time log signed by you and your mentor.
13. Verification of Mentoring Hours	Your mentor verifies the time he/she spent with you and the work done to complete your senior project product. You must include a scanned copy of this form signed by your mentor.
14. Mentor Evaluation Rubric	This is your mentor's opportunity to evaluate your work over the course of the creation of your product. You must include a scanned copy of the mentor evaluation rubric signed by your mentor.
15. Self-Evaluation Reflection	This is your final reflection, which is a summative reflection and self-evaluation of your entire senior project experience.

Senior project rubrics:

Note that each component is assessed as it is completed. The sign of commitment, project proposal, mentor evaluation, research paper, and presentation are evaluated with rubrics. Other components are assessed as "approved" or "not approved."

Source: Narragansett High School, Narragansett, Rhode Island. Used with permission.

FIGURE A.18 | **Quest Tour and Rubric**

Planner	Please describe your quest:
	1) What is the essential question guiding your quest?
	2) Please provide a mission statement for this quest. This should describe:
	• What you plan to do.
	• What you plan to deliver.
	• How long you think this will take.
	3) What is the genre of this quest?
	• Topical (a quest for information)
	• Issue-based (a quest to explore an issue)
	• Problem-based (a quest to solve a problem)
	• Thematic (a quest to connect ideas)
	• Case study (a quest to pursue skills or knowledge in depth)
	4) What is the scale of this quest?
	• Global
	• Local
	• Personal/Imaginative
Badges	By completing this quest, what badges do you hope to earn?
	Schoolwide:
	• Reading
	• Writing
	• Speaking
	• Mathematics
	• Technology
	• Civics/social studies
	• Science
	• Arts
	• Second language
	Personal Interest Badges:
	• Include any badges from your personal interest list that this quest will help you achieve.
	What habits of mind will you address on this quest?
	• Please list at least one habit of mind that you will focus on.
Resources/Network	As part of your quest, you will gain new skills and knowledge. Please include links below to any resources you have used to help you on your quest.
Deliverables	Please upload the artifacts you have created for this quest.
Reflection	How does this quest demonstrate that you have earned the selected badges?

(continued)

FIGURE A.18 | **Quest Tour and Rubric—(*continued*)**

Quest Rubric:

	4 - Exceeds Expectations	3 - Meets Expectations	2 - Needs More Work	1 - Needs More Instruction	0 - Does not apply
Completion: Tour includes all required elements					
Schoolwide Badge 1					
Schoolwide Badge 2					
Personal Interest Badge					
Habits of Mind Badge					

References

Alcock, M., Fisher, M., & Zmuda, A. (2018). *The quest for learning: How to maximize student engagement.* Bloomington, IN: Solution Tree Press.

Allen, D., & Blythe, T. (2004). *The facilitator's book of questions.* New York: Teachers College Press.

American Council on the Teaching of Foreign Languages (ACTFL). (2015). *World-readiness standards for learning language.* Retrieved from https://www.actfl.org/sites/default/files/publications/standards/World-ReadinessStandardsforLearningLanguages.pdf

Aprill, A. (2010). Direct instruction vs. arts integration: A false dichotomy. *Teaching Artist Journal, 8*(1), 6–15.

Brookhart, S. B. (2013). *How to create and use rubrics for formative assessment and grading.* Alexandria, VA: ASCD.

Coalition for Access, Affordability, and Success. (2016). www.coalitionforcollegeaccess.org

Costa, A. L., & Kallick, B. (Eds.). (2008). *Learning and leading with habits of mind: 16 essential characteristics for success.* Alexandria, VA: ASCD.

Danielson, C. (2007). *Enhancing professional practice: A framework for teaching* (2nd ed.). Alexandria, VA: ASCD.

Darling-Hammond, L. (2014, January/February). Testing to, and beyond, the Common Core. *Principal,* 10–12.

Darling-Hammond, L., Ancess, J., & Falk, B. (1995). *Authentic assessment in action.* New York: Teachers College Press.

Dewey, J. (1986). *How we think.* In J.A. Boydston (Ed.), *The later works of John Dewey, Volume 8, 1925–1953: 1933, Essays and how we think.* Carbondale, IL: University of Southern Illinois Press.

DiMartino, J. A., & Wolk, D. L. (Eds.). (2010). *The personalized high school: Making learning count for adolescents.* San Francisco: Jossey-Bass.

Duhigg, C. (2016). *Smarter faster better: The transformative power of real productivity.* New York: Random House.

Easton, L. B. (2009). *Protocols for professional learning.* Alexandria, VA: ASCD.

Education Northwest. (2014). Traits rubric for grades 3–12. Retrieved from http://educationnorthwest.org/sites/default/files/new-rubrics-3-12.pdf

Edutopia. (2011). The 40 reflection questions. Retrieved from https://www.edutopia.org/pdfs/stw/edutopia-stw-replicatingPBL-21stCAcad-reflection-questions.pdf

Exemplars. (2017). Instructional task: Grade 4. Retrieved from https://www.exemplars.com/education-materials/free-samples/pscc-4-instruction

Fishman, B., Teasley, S., & Cederquist, S. (2018). *Micro-credentials as evidence for college readiness: Report of an NSF workshop.* Ann Arbor, MI: University of Michigan.

Fullan, M. (2015). *The new meaning of educational change* (5th ed.). New York: Teachers College Press.

Grant, S. L. (2014). *What counts as learning: Open digital badges for new opportunities.* Irvine, CA: Digital Media and Learning Research Hub.

Hannaford-Agor, P., Hans, V. P., Mott, N. L., & Munsterman, G. T. (2004, July). Why do hung juries hang? *NIJ Journal, 251,* 25–27. Retrieved from https://www.ncjrs.gov/pdffiles1/jr000251h.pdf

Hirsch, E. D. (1987). *Cultural literacy: What every American needs to know.* New York: Houghton Mifflin.

Hoerr, T. R. (2017). *The formative five: Fostering grit, empathy, and other success skills every student needs.* Alexandria, VA: ASCD.

Hurwitz, M., & Lee, J. (2018). Grade inflation and the role of standardized testing. In J. Buckley, L. Letukas, & B. Wildavsky (Eds.), *Measuring success: Testing, grades, and the future of college admissions* (pp. 64–93). Baltimore: Johns Hopkins University Press.

International Baccalaureate Organization. (2017). How the PYP works. Retrieved from http://www.ibo.org/programmes/primary-years-programme/what-is-the-pyp/how-the-pyp-works

International Society for Technology in Education. (2016). *ISTE standards for students.* Retrieved from http://www.iste.org/standards/for-students

Jacobs, H. H. (Ed.). (2004). *Getting results with curriculum mapping.* Alexandria, VA: ASCD.

Jacobs, H. H. (Ed.). (2010). *Curriculum 21: Essential education for a changing world.* Alexandria, VA: ASCD.

Jacobs, H. H., & Alcock, M. H. (2017). *Bold moves for schools: How we create remarkable learning environments.* Alexandria, VA: ASCD.

Jung, L. A. (2018). Scales of progress. *Educational Leadership, 75*(5), 23–27.

Kallick, B., & Zmuda, A. (2017). *Students at the center: Personalized learning with habits of mind.* Alexandria, VA: ASCD.

Larmer, J., Mergendoller, J. R., & Boss, S. (2015a). *Gold standard PBL: Essential project design elements.* Novato, CA: Buck Institute for Education. Retrieved from http://www.bie.org/blog/gold_standard_pbl_essential_project_design_elements

Larmer, J., Mergendoller, J. R., & Boss, S. (2015b). *Setting the standard for project based learning: A proven approach to rigorous instruction.* Alexandria, VA: ASCD; Novato, CA: Buck Institute for Education.

McDonald, J. (1992). Dilemmas of planning backwards: Rescuing a good idea. *Teachers College Record, 94*(1), 152–169.

McDonald, J. P., Mohr, N., Dichter, A., & McDonald, E. C. (2013). *The power of protocols: An educator's guide to better practice* (3rd ed.). New York: Teachers College Press.

McDonald, J. P., Smith, S., Turner, D., Finney, M., & Barton, E. (1993). *Graduation by exhibition: Assessing genuine achievement*. Alexandria, VA: ASCD.

McTighe, J. (2017). Designing cornerstone tasks to promote meaningful learning and assess what matters most [handout]. Retrieved from https://dpi.wi.gov/sites/default/files/imce/ela/resources/McTighe_Handout_2%5B1%5D.pdf

McTighe, J. (2018). Three key questions on measuring learning. *Educational Leadership*, *75*(5), 14–20.

Meier, D. (2002). *In schools we trust: Creating communities of learning in an era of testing and standardization*. Boston: Beacon Press.

Narragansett High School. (2014). *Narragansett High School senior project manual*. Retrieved from http://www.nhs.nssk12.org/cms/One.aspx?portalId=203964&pageId=613635

National Council of Teachers of Mathematics. (2000). *Principles and standards for school mathematics*. Retrieved from https://www.nctm.org/standards

NGSS Lead States. (2013). *Next Generation Science Standards: For states, by states*. Appendix G: Crosscutting concepts. Washington, DC: National Academies Press. Retrieved from http://www.nextgenscience.org/sites/default/files/Appendix%20G%20-%20Crosscutting%20Concepts%20FINAL%20edited%204.10.13.pdf

National Governors Association Center for Best Practices, Council of Chief State School Officers. (2010). *Common Core State Standards for English language arts and literacy in history/social studies, science, and technical subjects*. Washington DC: Author.

Niguidula, D. (1993). *The digital portfolio: A richer picture of student performance. Studies on exhibitions (No. 13.)*. Providence, RI: Coalition of Essential Schools.

Niguidula, D. (1997). Picturing performance with digital portfolios. *Educational Leadership*, *55*(3), 26–29.

Niguidula, D. (2006). Whose portfolio is it, anyway? Implementing digital portfolios in K–12 schools. In A. Jafari & C. Kaufman (Eds.), *Handbook of research on ePortfolios* (pp. 496–502). Hershey, PA: Idea Group Reference.

Niguidula, D. (2010). Digital portfolios and curriculum maps: Linking student and teacher work. In H. H. Jacobs (Ed.), *Curriculum 21: Essential education for a changing world* (pp. 153–167). Alexandria, VA: ASCD.

Niguidula, D. (2015). Digital teacher portfolios. In L. Easton (Ed.), *Powerful designs for professional learning* (3rd ed.). Oxford, OH: National Staff Development Council.

Office of Innovation, State of Rhode Island. (2016). *Creating a shared understanding of personalized learning for Rhode Island*. Providence, RI: Office of Innovation, State of Rhode Island.

Ohio Department of Education. (2017). Standards for mathematical practice. Retrieved from https://education.ohio.gov/Topics/Learning-in-Ohio/Mathematics/Model-Curricula-in-Mathematics/Standards-for-Mathematical-Practice

Ontario Ministry of Education. (2010). Growing success: Assessment, evaluation, and reporting in Ontario schools. Retrieved from http://www.edu.gov.on.ca/eng/policy-funding/growSuccess.pdf

Papert, S. (1980). *Mindstorms: Children, computers, and powerful ideas*. New York: Basic Books.

Renwick, M. (2017). *Digital portfolios in the classroom: Showcasing and assessing student work*. Alexandria, VA: ASCD.

Riconscente, M. M., Kamarainen, A., & Honey, M. (2013). *STEM badges: Current terrain and the road ahead.* New York: New York Hall of Science.

Sarason, S. (1996). *Revising "The culture of the school and the problem of change."* New York: Teachers College Press.

Stanford Center for Assessment, Learning, and Equity [SCALE]. (2017). SCALE Checklist for quality rubric design. Retrieved from https://www.performanceassessmen-tresourcebank.org/resource/10481

Senge, P., Cambron-McCabe, N., Lucas, T., Smith, B., Dutton. J., & Kleiner, A. (2012). *Schools that learn* (2nd ed.). New York: Crown Business.

Sizer, T. R. (1992). *Horace's school: Redesigning the American high school.* New York: Houghton Mifflin.

Stiggins, R. (2017). *The perfect assessment system.* Alexandria, VA: ASCD.

Van Noorden, R. (2014, May 7). Global scientific output doubles every nine years [blog post]. Retrieved from nature.com at http://blogs.nature.com/news/2014/05/global-sci-entific-output-doubles-every-nine-years.html

Wagner, T. (2008). *The global achievement gap: Why even our best schools don't teach the new survival skills our children need—and what we can do about it.* New York: Basic Books.

Webb, N. L. (2002). *Depth-of-knowledge levels for four content areas.* Retrieved from http://facstaff.wcer.wisc.edu/normw/All%20content%20areas%20%20DOK%20levels%2032802.pdf

Wiggins, G. (1989). The futility of trying to teach everything of importance. *Educational Leadership, 47*(3), 44–48, 57–59.

Wiggins, G. (1998). *Educative assessment: Designing assessments to inform and improve student performance.* San Francisco: Jossey-Bass.

Wiggins, G., & McTighe, J. (2011). *The Understanding by Design guide to creating high-quality units.* Alexandria, VA: ASCD.

Xia, R. (2017, August 3). Cal State will no longer require placement exams and remedial classes for freshmen. *Los Angeles Times.* Retrieved from http://www.latimes.com/local/lanow/la-me-cal-state-remedial-requirements-20170803-story.html

Zmuda, A., Curtis, G., & Ullman, D. (2015). *Learning personalized: The evolution of the contemporary classroom.* San Francisco: Jossey-Bass.

Index

The letter *f* following a page number denotes a figure.

About the Author

 **David Niguidula,** EdD, is founder of Ideas Consulting, based in Providence, Rhode Island. He is best known for his work on digital portfolios in K–12 schools; in the 1990s, Niguidula led the first research project on the topic while at Brown University's Coalition of Essential Schools. Through his development of the Richer Picture platform, Niguidula has assisted schools and districts across the country and around the world as they create proficiency-based requirements and implement new assessment practices.

Niguidula's focus is on using technology for transforming school practice. He has published articles and led workshops for numerous publications, including ASCD's *Educational Leadership*.

Prior to joining the Coalition of Essential Schools, Niguidula worked on educational technology projects at the Institute for Mathematics and Science Education Development (ISMED) at the University of the Philippines, Diliman, and at the Educational Technology Center at the Harvard Graduate School of Education.

Niguidula has degrees in computer science and education from Brown University and earned his doctorate in instructional technology and media at Teachers College, Columbia University.

He can be reached at david@ideasconsulting.com and at www.richerpicture.com.

Acknowledgments

This book is a distillation of nearly 30 years of building an idea. When I first started introducing the concept of digital portfolios in the early 1990s, many schools were just beginning to think about using e-mail and trying to figure out how to budget enough for floppy disks. While the technology has changed rapidly, the ideas have taken shape at their own pace. The effective use of digital badges and portfolios for mastery has been a joint undertaking of educators, researchers, and advisors; the power of these concepts has emerged through countless hours of classroom practice and conversations with colleagues. Through the years, many people have contributed generously with their thoughts, with their time, and with their efforts.

As an undergraduate at Brown University, I was fortunate to work with two mentors in both departments of my double major: Andries van Dam in computer science and Theodore Sizer in education. Both are pioneering visionaries in their respective fields. When Sam Matsa of the IBM Foundation proposed a collaboration between technology and school reform, Andy and Ted brought me in as a translator between the two departments. This eventually became the Exhibitions Project at Brown's Coalition of Essential Schools and led to the initial research on digital portfolios. I will always be grateful for the opportunity Andy and Ted gave me, and for their belief that a twenty-something could make a significant contribution to the field.

The early work on portfolios came to life when colleagues in schools were willing to put brand-new ideas into practice. Sherry King, Kathy Mason, Paul Allison, Nancy Mohr, Eileen Barton, Scott Horan, Dennis Littky, Rick Durkee, Tom Warner, and so many others were exemplars in showing the world that school change is not just possible but can thrive in the right settings. The Exhibitions Group at the Coalition, led by Joe McDonald and including David Allen and Jody Brown Podl, was instrumental in keeping the focus on the new possibilities for assessment and many other aspects of school change. Michelle Riconscente was my partner through the key years of this work, providing technical expertise and a sounding board for figuring out what would work best for schools. The extraordinary community of colleagues at the Coalition, including Paula Evans, Rick Lear, Pat Wasley, Sue Lusi, Jill Davidson, Bob McCarthy, Stan Thompson, Bev Simpson, Gene Thompson-Grove, and Larry Myatt, helped over the years just by sharing their thoughts and taking the time to listen.

I have also been able to find support in the academic, state, and education innovation communities that help put the work on digital portfolios and badges in the larger context. Jan Hawkins, Margaret Honey, Linda Darling-Hammond, Viv White, Rick Richards, Colleen Callahan, Peter McWalters, Alan November, Bob Pearlman, Robbie McClintock, Hugh (Tony) Cline, David Ruff, Van Schoales, Barry Fishman, Hilarie Davis, Scott Brown, Janet Hale, Bill Sheskey, Mike Fisher, Jeanne Tribuzzi, Marie Alcock, and Allison Zmuda have all extended their incredible expertise and insights.

I am particularly honored that three icons in the field have provided guidance, encouragement and support for these endeavors. Heidi Hayes Jacobs, Jay McTighe, and Bena Kallick have long been public advocates for my work on digital portfolios, and they were all kind enough to respond to early drafts of this manuscript. Heidi graciously wrote the foreword, and our frequent collaborations always leave me enlightened and energized. Each of them has influenced a generation with their groundbreaking contributions to teaching and learning, and I am very appreciative that they have been champions for my ideas.

More recent implementations of digital portfolios and badges have only been possible because of educators dedicated to the true meaning of personalization—helping all students achieve at their highest potential: Joe Maruszczak, David Moscarelli, Paula Faria, Mary Keable, Dave Meoli, Ann Croft, Denise Bilodeau, Katie Miller, Cheryl August, Yasmina Thomas, Betty Durfee, Danielle Parrillo, Marco Andrade, Kris Klenk, Sharon Ayala, Josh Goodwin, Hazel Joseph-Roseboro, Paul Woods, Steve Murphy, Kim Carter, Elizabeth Cardine, Mike Barnes, Jennifer Hiro, Sarah Brumberg, Scott Brown, Victor Capellan, Elizabeth Ochs, Stacia Jackson, Tom Hoffman, KC Perry, Bill Carozza, Susan Wood, Jackie Vetrovec, Marianne Greenwood,

Patricia McLoughlin, Megan Baker, John O'Brien, Phil Price, Paul Dalpe, Georgia Fortunato, Kevin McNamara, Cynthia Schneider, Kristin Frunzi, Nancy Maguire-Heath, Barbara Cesana, Bill Wehrli, Julie Anne Levin, Jodi Anthony, and Mike Rulon.

In addition, to keep up with the changing technologies, I am indebted to the work of a fantastic team of software developers and technical support staff who have contributed so much over the years to the Richer Picture tools.

In preparing this manuscript, I want to thank the editorial staff at ASCD and especially Allison Scott and Liz Wegner who saw this project through its many stages. Thanks to Goldylyn Visaya for creating many of the illustrations (including the badges).

Finally, the most valuable support has come from home. My parents had an unwavering faith in me and instilled the notion that working for others is the best way to share one's light. Gregory and Carlene have grown up with this work, and being the parent to two wonderful young adults is the privilege of a lifetime. And, most of all, this work is dedicated to Reina, whose unwavering faith, hope, sacrifice, encouragement, cajoling, humor, and love have allowed me to fulfill my dreams—and who has always shown that the best collaborations are those where everyone grows.

Related ASCD Resources

At the time of publication, the following resources were available (ASCD stock numbers in parentheses).

Print Products

Bold Moves for Schools: How We Create Remarkable Learning Environments by Heidi Hayes Jacobs and Marie Hubley Alcock (#115013)

Curriculum 21: Essential Education for a Changing World edited by Heidi Hayes Jacobs (#109008)

Digital Portfolios in the Classroom: Showcasing and Assessing Student Work by Matt Renwick (#117005)

How to Give Effective Feedback to Your Students, 2nd Edition by Susan M. Brookhart (#116066)

Project Based Teaching: How to Create Rigorous and Engaging Learning Experiences by Suzie Boss with John Larmer (#118047)

Students at the Center: Personalized Learning with Habits of Mind by Bena Kallick and Allison Zmuda (#117015)

Tasks Before Apps: Designing Rigorous Learning in a Tech-Rich Classroom by Monica Burns (#118019)

ASCD myTeachSource®

Download resources from a professional learning platform with hundreds of research-based best practices and tools for your classroom at http://myteach-source.ascd.org/

For more information, send an e-mail to member@ascd.org; call 1-800-933-2723 or 703-578-9600; send a fax to 703-575-5400; or write to Information Services, ASCD, 1703 N. Beauregard St., Alexandria, VA 22311-1714 USA.

THE WHOLE CHILD

The ASCD Whole Child approach is an effort to transition from a focus on narrowly defined academic achievement to one that promotes the long-term development and success of all children. Through this approach, ASCD supports educators, families, community members, and policymakers as they move from a vision about educating the whole child to sustainable, collaborative actions.

Demonstrating Student Mastery with Digital Badges and Portfolios relates to the **engaged**, **supported**, *and* **challenged** *tenets. For more about the ASCD Whole Child approach, visit* **www.ascd.org/ wholechild.**

WHOLE CHILD
TENETS

① HEALTHY
Each student enters school healthy and learns about and practices a healthy lifestyle.

② SAFE
Each student learns in an environment that is physically and emotionally **safe** for students and adults.

③ ENGAGED
Each student is actively engaged in learning and is connected to the school and broader community.

④ SUPPORTED
Each student has access to personalized learning and is supported by qualified, caring adults.

⑤ CHALLENGED
Each student is challenged academically and prepared for success in college or further study and for employment and participation in a global environment.

Become an ASCD member today!
Go to www.ascd.org/joinascd
or call toll-free: 800-933-ASCD (2723)

LEARN. TEACH. LEAD.